THE CRITICAL PATH

FROM THE BIG BANG

TO

THE MESSIANIC AGE

By

Chaim Wolff

The Critical Path – *From the Big Bang to the Messianic Age*

The Critical Path – From the Big Bang to the Messianic Age
By Chaim Wolff © 2016

ISBN: 1539657302

Published by: Create Space Publishing

NOTE FROM THE AUTHOR

A comprehensive understanding of where we are, how we got here and where we need to be is best accomplished with some knowledge of the 'Big Bang", the distribution of matter in space, the evolution of our species, our country's history and religious wisdom. This wisdom must be understood without dogma or threat to others who are not committed to killing us first. Otherwise self-defense must prevail. Our history proves we have always acted in humanity's best interest.

We are a true melting pot "with liberty and justice for all". Our religious freedom has enabled every religion, color and race to be their best and the worst. Our Civil War prove our willingness to fight for justice and our world wars proved our willingness to fight for freedom. Islam is guilty of indifference and therefore irrelevance in the pursuit of peace and ISIS has become the modern day Amalek , justifying complete and total destruction.

3

Religious truths from the time of Jesus pave the path to the messianic age. These are evident in the Bar Ilan writings handed down by every generation of rabbis since 500 A.D. these should be codified and encoded in "Big Blue" thereby enabling the creation of a modern Sanhedrin. Seventy two respected leaders should be impaneled to advise our government thereby.

Our foreign policy must consider the threat of Islamic and leftists' alliances which surround us and threaten all of Europe and Israel. These are supported by the UN and should be removed from the US. Our embassy should immediately be moved to Jerusalem, which should be declared the capital of a United Jewish state between the mountains and the sea. Our embassy should immediately be moved to Jerusalem.

Finally, there is reason to hope for a paradigm shift in energy, which will enable "feeding the hungry, clothing the naked and providing "sweet water" anywhere. 1000 years of peace awaits a strong, rearmed, United America. President Trump and the Republican Party will lead the way!

Chaim Wolff

TABLE OF CONTENTS

CHAPTER 1

An Insight

According to Rep. Paul Ryan, "Yuval Levin is one of the most insightful and original thinkers of our time". When it comes to describing the nature of the problems confronting us I am inclined to agree. Mr. Levin says, "The social democratic vision begins with the observation that capitalism, while capable of producing great prosperity, leaves many people profoundly insecure. This fact suggests to social Democrats that the functioning of the market economy should be strictly controlled by a system of robust regulations, and that its effects should be softened by a system of robust social insurance. From birth to death, citizens should be ensconced in the series of protections and benefits: universal childcare, universal healthcare, universal public schooling and higher education, welfare benefits for the poor, generous labor protections for workers. Dexterous management of the levers of the economy ease the cycles of boom and bust, skillful direction of public funds to spur private productivity and efficiency. Each would be overseen by a competent and rational bureaucracy, and the whole would make for a system that is not only beneficent but unifying and dignifying, and one that enables the pursuit of common national goals while also liberating individuals from oppressive social structures and from a crippling material dependence on family and community. (pgs. 130, 131)

In public policy, market oriented solutions would mean that, instead of trying to address complex problems with uniform programs imposed in a centralized way, we would allow an assortment of potential problem solvers (public and private local regional and national) to propose or attempt various solutions in different circumstances. (pgs. 133, 134)

While this has already proven not to work within our current political system, this speaks directly to the Jewish biblical solution using local "Sanhedrin's" to solve our social problems and bring us back to our religious roots so threatened by the tower of Babel in which we live.

Seven books define the problem: "Constantine's Sword" by James Carrol,[1] "A World Lit Only By Fire" by William Manchester[2], "America's Prophet" by Bruce Feiler[3], "The Spirit of Democratic Capitalism" by Michael Novak[4], "The Great Deformation" by David A. Stockman[5] and "The Arab Mind" by Raphael Patai[6].

Typically, unintended consequences undermine efforts to correct problems. Trying to limit taxable pay to $1 million a year, itself not a bad idea as per President Jimmy Carter, led almost immediately to the creation of the stock option the Black Sholes equation and "The Big Short" as unintended consequences. It weakened the connection between the stockholders, the executives, the owners and employees. Now executives making 500 to 1000 times entry-level wages have distorted the equitable distribution of wealth and have given too small a minority the benefits of what we all produce. God-given

---

[1] Constantine's Sword by James Carroll
[2] A World Lit Only by Fire by William Manchester
[3] America's Prophet by Bruce Feiler
[4] The Spirit of Democratic Capitalism by Michael Novak
[5] The Great Deformation" by David A. Stockman
[6] The Arab Mind" by Raphael Patai.

intelligence is what separates the wealthy from the worker and is not the best measure of one's value. Executives in the 1970s made 100-200 times the entry-level wage and most of us worked hard because we were all in it together. Now there is little sensibility and a 55-year-old employee may be laid off to save the added cost of his retirement. No sense of responsibility or justice limits the perverse decision to fire rather than reduce all pay to preserve jobs.

Further, the computer age has turned all of its potential to improve the quality of life primarily into greater productivity. Now we can be connected even during the most private and intimate moments and yet only top executive pay keeps increasing while productivity has increased. Dramatically increased computer capacity has enabled the most complicated formulas for pricing options, leading to extreme financial leveraging, which caused the financial crisis and is threatening another. The infamous Black Sholes equation enabled the calculation of option prices for deals which make no business sense. Bundled with good mortgages, bad mortgages resulted in some ventures being leveraged more than 1000 to 1. Failure was inevitable.

"We have to pass it to know what is in it" referencing the health care fiasco and "What difference does it make" regarding the deaths of Embassy staff clearly describes the "tyranny of arrogance" increasingly threatening our political and national integrity. Our learned scholars have continued to know more and more about less and less and seem to have forgotten the questions.

As a result, recent history shows us to be moving down "the road to serfdom"[7]. Frederick A. Hayek was a co-winner of the Nobel Prize for economics in 1974 for his classic warning about the dangers to freedom inherent in social planning. While he was writing about his native England in the book "The Road to Serfdom" he is describing our current America. We would have done well to heed his concerns. Perhaps it would have minimized "The Corruption of Capitalism in America" as described by David A. Stockman in his seminal book "The Great Deformation". The financial collapse of 2008 was the direct result of stupid economic math and stupid government regulation and it is about to happen again.

---

[7] The Road to Serfdom by Frederick A. Hayek

Senators Dodd and Frank were the primary perpetrators then and will be the same now. Their legislation is so convoluted as to defy understanding. It can be interpreted to mean whatever you want. It seems to be a level of human nature, that it is easier for people to agree with the largest group of people whose values are similar to those of people with low standards. The lowest common denominator unites the largest number of people. As per Hayek, our concern should be that majority democratic government might be as oppressive as the worst dictatorship. If it undertook to centrally direct the economic system, it would probably destroy personal freedom as completely as any autocracy has ever done! And so, it has!

*****

In the present case, the critical path began with "The Big Bang" 13.7 billion years ago. It required the creation of trillions of stars, billions of galaxies and will end with the Messianic Age at the Jewish year 6000, 226 years from now. Should our government elect to follow this plan 1000 years of peace should follow. Otherwise, we might expect governance by Tweet; the 140-character expression, which seems to sum up the knowledge of the generation which made it eminent. Frankly I'm sick of it!

Our political system is on the verge of self-destruction. We cannot carry on any civil conversation and we are fiddling while our country is burning. As you should have learned from the prior discussion there is a way of belief which has been honed by history and is now ignored by its inheritors which accurately describes the problems in governance. Hayek suggests that there is no complete ethical code to be used as a guide. Hayek is wrong! That guide is contained in the Bar Ilan papers[8], which include the commentary of religious Jews since about 500 CE through the present day. These commentaries discuss how best to make God's word eminent. They pertain not only to Jews but to all mankind.

Devoid of dogma their message provides a path to peace enabling each to achieve their potential without fear or threat from the other. By way of example a well-known principle of Jewish law requires "leaving the corner of the field" to the workers to be gleaned by the poor and hungry. A contemporary version of this law might allow corporations to allocate 25% of their profits for social welfare programs to be administered by

---

[8] Bar Ilan papers

their own employees. This instead of paying taxes to the government will ensure that social programs are being administered closer to their recipients and in direct response to their requirements. Campaign financing should be limited to a maximum of $100 million, to minimize corporate or private influence on our elected officials. Term limits should become mandatory and retirement benefits adjusted accordingly. Maybe this is a stretch but in the right direction.

A substantially increased minimum wage ($15/hr.) could be funded by a modest increase in the cost of goods whereby all would benefit. Funding the increased benefit by reducing corporate pay might be a good way to reconcile the inequity created by stock options. These were a mistake to begin with thanks to Pres. Jimmy Carter's attempt to limit corporate salaries. When I was working for Shell, our top executive made 250 times our entry-level pay. Now 1000 times entry-level pay is not too much for self-serving executives with closely related boards of directors. God given intelligence is what separates the few from the many and does not justify such exorbitant waste of corporate resources.

Political contributions have caused government to pursue nefarious schemes related to unproven science, ignoring natural laws and the science of creation itself. By way of contrast, "Focus Fusion", which recently received limited endorsement by four of the more important scientists of our time including the former head of the Energy Research and Development Administration (ERDA), has received virtually no government funding despite overwhelming published proof of its potential benefits. The reader is encouraged to learn more from the Lawrenceville plasma physics website. (I am a stockholder and a member of their board of advisors.)

In any case, current religious models fail contemporary needs and only by return to the roots which Jesus never left will society be able to build a model of religious practice capable of bringing us to an age of peace.

IBM's "Watson" needs to be programmed with everything there is to know about everything knowable, including the Bar Ilan discussions reflecting 3000 years of religious teachings and all the major sciences. Then we need to empanel a new Sanhedrin of 72 selected citizens to input the questions and evaluate the answers.

"The righteous beholding this will rejoice, the upright will be glad, the pious will celebrate with song when you remove the tyranny of arrogance from the earth". (Mahzor Lev Shalom, p. 13)

CHAPTER 2
Democratic Capitalism

The Wall Street Journal described Novak's book[9] as "the most remarkable and original treatise on the roots of modern capitalism to be published in many years". He concludes, "No intelligent human order-not even within the church bureaucracy-can be run according to the councils of Christianity. Not even saints and company assembled can bear such a regimen. A free economy cannot be a Christian economy... And cooperate in coalitions where consensus may be reached. (pg. 352)

But it could be a capitalistic economy built upon Jewish economic principles as I hope you will come to understand. The task is enormous because of the economic disparities which have been exacerbated by political influence, lobbying, greed, and corruption. The decontrol begun under President Reagan was well-meaning to begin, but it became a vehicle to benefit fewer and fewer as it became the criteria that directed its

---

[9] The Spirit of Democratic Capitalism by Michael Novak

implementation. Executives making 500 to 1000 times entry-level wages have prevented the equitable distribution of wealth and have made the beneficiaries too few.

God given intelligence is what should separate the wealthy from the worker and is not the best measure of one's worth. Now there is little sense of loyalty and a 55-year-old employee may be laid off to save the added cost of his or her retirement. No sense of responsibility or justice limits the perverse decision to lay off rather than to reduce all pay to preserve jobs. The computer age has turned on all of its potential to improve the quality of life, primarily into greater productivity.

Now we can be connected even during our most private and intimate moments and yet, all but top executive pay has remained level for years while productivity has increased dramatically. Only misplaced values are so indifferent to the plight of the working class.

Michael Novak believes as I that "political democracy is compatible in practice only with the market economy" (pg14). We agree that the State which does not recognize limits to its power in the economic sphere inevitably destroys liberties in the political sphere. This is well underway and threatens our very way of life. A democratic system depends for its legitimacy not upon equal results but upon a sense of equal opportunity. Novak describes Democratic capitalism as three systems in one: a predominantly market economy; a polity respectful of the rights of the individual to life, liberty and the pursuit of happiness; and a system of cultural institutions built by ideals of liberty and justice for all. (pg. 14)

According to Novak, "In the conventional view political democracy is compatible in practice only with a market economy. History has proven that planned systems, communism and socialism flow from the subjection of each citizen by the state. Democratic capitalism combines the predominantly market economy with a polity respectful of the human rights of the individual to life, liberty and the pursuit of happiness and a system of cultural institutions moved by ideals of liberty and justice for all."

In turn a pluralistic, liberal culture is important to give attention to all three systems… To begin with, modern democracy and modern capitalism proceed from identical historical impulses. These impulses had moral form before institutions were invented to limit the power of the State, in defense against tyranny and stagnation; and to liberate the energies of individuals and independently organized communities."

The natural logic of capitalism leads to democracy, for economic liberties without political liberties are inherently unstable. Citizens economically free soon demand political freedoms. Most importantly Democratic polities depend on the reality of economic growth. No socialist society, indeed no society in history, has ever produced strict equality among individuals or classes. Real differences in talent, aspiration and application inexorably individuate humans. We are as different mentally as we are physically and to level the playing field changes the rules entirely and it is not in the best interest for our country. Given the diversity of human life an economic system cannot possibly guarantee equal outcomes or even something for nothing. A democratic system depends for its legitimacy therefore not upon equal results but upon a sense of equal opportunity. Liberated by economic growth democracy wins common consent.

Not only do the logic of democracy and the logic of the market economy strengthen one another, both also require a special moral cultural base. Without this and certain cultural presuppositions about the nature of individuals and their communities about liberty and sin; about the changeability of history; about work and savings; about self-restraint and mutual cooperation; neither democracy nor capitalism can be made to work. (pg. 16)

We are there now! $17,000,000,000,000 in national debt is an unconscionable burden which profligate spending has placed upon future generations. It is imperative that we step back from the path we are on and return to our religious roots and capitalistic economy. This is essential because only ideas of enormous cruelty and impracticality retain the allegiance of the elites that benefit from them. Those elites include long-standing members of our political establishment, high wealth business owners and others, comprising less than 1% of our total population.

In a world of instantaneous universal mass communications, the balance of power has now shifted. Ideas always a part of reality have today acquired power greater than that of reality. One of the most astonishing characteristics of our age is that ideas even false and unworkable ideas, even ideas which are no longer believed in by their official guarantor guardians, rule the affairs of man and run roughshod over stubborn facts. Ideas of enormous destructiveness, cruelty and impracticality, retain the allegiance of the elites that benefit from them. The empirical record seems not to jump through into consciousness to break their spell. The class of persons who earn their livelihood from the making of ideas and symbols seems both unusually bewitched by falsehoods and absurdities and uniquely empowered to impose upon them and impose them upon hapless individuals. (pgs. 19, 20)

Not only do the logic of democracy and the logic of the market economy strengthen one another, both also require a special moral cultural base. Without certain moral and cultural presuppositions about the nature of individuals and their communities, about liberty and about the changeability of history, about work and savings, about self-restraint and mutual cooperation, neither democracy nor capitalism can be made to work.

Pope Pius XI said that the tragedy of the 19th century was the loss of the working classes to the church and even deeper tragedy lay in the failure of the church to understand the moral cultural roots of the new economics. Attached to the past the church did not leaven the new order. Michael Novak gives too much credit to Christianity. The sordid history of anti-Semitism still prevalent today and Pope Francis' bias toward the Palestinians and his ignorance of Jewish history disqualifies him from any constructive role in solving our economic problems. In a world of instantaneous universal mass communications, the balance of power has now shifted. Ideas, as encompassed in the 140-character tweet, tell this generation everything it cares to know about how to solve our political and economic problems.

The tweet has resulted in one of the most astonishing characteristics of our age. Ideas even false and unworkable ideas which are no longer believed in by their official guardians rule the affairs of man and run roughshod over stubborn facts. Ideas of enormous destructiveness, cruelty and impracticality retain the allegiance of the elites that benefit from their empirical record but which seem not to jump through into consciousness to break their spell. The class of persons who earn their livelihood from the making of ideas and symbols seems both unusually bewitched by falsehoods and absurdities and uniquely empowered to impose them upon hapless individuals, thus the audacity of hope is crushed by the tyranny of arrogance.

As Novak explains Democratic capitalism seems to have lost its spirit. Its Achilles' heel is that for two centuries now it has appealed so little to the human spirit. If the system in which we live is better than any theory about the guardians of the spirits, poets and philosophers and priests have not penetrated to its secret springs, they have neither deciphered its spiritual wisdom, they have not loved their own culture. (pg. 31)

The ironic flaw in capitalism is that its successes in the political order and in the economic order and in the cultural order is that the more it succeeds, the more it fails. Here are a few of the most commonly heard indictments:

(1) The corruption of affluence. Moral discipline yields successes. But the success corrupts moral discipline. Citizens desire something for nothing- and they get it.

(2) Advertising and moral weakness. The leaders of the economic system permit advertising to appeal to the worst in citizens. They encourage credit card debt, convenience purchasing, the loosening of restraint. This is reflected in the modern television show Mad Men, which was about the advertising industry in New York, during the time when I was working in the oil fields in West Texas and smoking three packs a day.

(3) The leaders of the political order take advantage of a structural weakness in all democratic societies. Unable to depend on strong political parties, political leaders face the people alone. Clothing themselves in symbolism and wishes, their promises of benefits become a special form of bribery endemic to democracy. Since each politician is on his own none has an institutional reason to worry about who will eventually pay the costs.

David A. Stockman in his epochal book "THE GREAT DEFORMATION" was of considerable influence in position's which enable him to clearly understand "The Corruption of

Capitalism in America" and its subsequent collapse in 2008 and its pending collapse in 2016.

What this has cost us is now reflected in our national debt estimated to be $17,000,000,000,000; coincidentally, more dollars than the number of light years since creation. In any case a very large number unconscionable for a democratic capitalistic society to have accumulated. According to the back flap of his book, David A. Stockman was elected as a Michigan congressman in 1976 and joined the Reagan White House in 1981. Serving as budget director, he was one of the key architects of the Reagan revolution plan to reduce taxes, cut spending and shrink the role of government. He joined Salomon Brothers in 1985 and later became one of the early partners of the Blackstone group. During nearly two decades at Blackstone and at a firm he founded, Stockman was a private equity investor. Stockman attended Michigan State University and Harvard Divinity School and then went to Washington as a congressional aide in 1970. He is also the author of the number one bestseller "The Triumph of Politics."

If you only read one book about where we are, and why, I recommend this one. The front piece of the book summarizes "The Great Deformation" as a searing look at Washington's craven response to the recent myriad of financial crises and fiscal cliffs. It counters conventional wisdom with an 80-year revisionist history of how the American state-especially the Federal Reserve- has fallen prey to the politics of crony capitalism and the ideologies of fiscal stimulus, monetary central planning, and financial bailouts. These forces have left the public-sector teetering on the edge of political dysfunction and fiscal collapse and have caused America's private enterprise foundation to morph into a speculative casino that swindles the masses and enriches the few.

Defying right and left wing boxes, David Stockman provides a catalog of corrupters and defenders of sound money, fiscal rectitude and free markets. The former includes: Franklin Roosevelt, who fathered crony capitalism; Richard Nixon, who destroyed national financial discipline and the Bretton Woods' Gold backed dollar; (a huge mistake) Fed Chairmen Greenspan and Bernanke, who fostered our present scourge of bubble finance and addiction to debt and speculation; George W. Bush, who repudiated fiscal rectitude and ballooned the warfare state via senseless wars; (Iraq was not senseless and had we stayed I do not believe ISIS would have become a force.) And Barack Obama, who revived failed "Keynesian borrow and spend" policies that have driven the national debt to perilous heights. By contrast, the book also traces a parade of statesman who championed balanced budgets and financial market discipline including Carter Glass, Harry Truman, Dwight Eisenhower, Bill Simon, Paul Volker, Bill Clinton, and Sheila Bair.

Stockman's analysis skewers Keynesian spenders and GOP tax-cutters, showing how they converged to bloat the welfare state, perpetuate the military-industrial complex and deplete the revenue base- even as the feds massive money printing allowed politicians to enjoy deficits without tears. But these policies have also fueled the financial bubbles, favoring Wall Street with cheap money and rigged stock and bond markets while crushing *Main Street* savers and punishing family budgets with soaring food and energy costs.

The Great Deformation explains how we got here and quantifies hapless policies which are an epochal threat to free market prosperity and American political democracy.

We are also confronted with 25 countries who are now proposing a new bundle of currencies to supplant the dollar. We are faced with economic chaos, political anarchy, social upheaval, Islamic fundamentalists, Black Lives that Don't Matter, Europe in turmoil and we are facing a threatening coalition of Iran, Syria, Iraq, Russia, China, North Korea, Pakistan and various South American countries, all surrounding North America. And yet the "tweet" goes on!

ON THAT DAY, THE LORD SHALL BE ONE AND HIS NAME ONE!

$17 trillion dollars of accumulated debt, most of it in the last eight years, proves that Democratic capitalism has lost its spirit and its appeal to the human spirit. Our leaders have not deciphered the spiritual wisdom of our economic system, nor taught its spiritual wisdom. According to Michael Novak in his book, *The Spirit of Democratic Capitalism*, the ironic flaw in capitalism is this: successes in the political order and in the economic order undermine it in the cultural order. The more it succeeds, the more it fails.

Here are a few of the most commonly heard indictments:

(1) "The corruption of affluence". Moral discipline yields successes, but success corrupts moral discipline.

(2)" Advertising and moral weakness." The leaders of the economic system permit advertising to appeal to the worst in citizens. They encourage credit card debt, convenience purchasing, the loosening of restraint, and as per "Mad Men" the smoking of three packs a day. (I was a drilling engineer in West Texas during those times and did in fact smoke three packs a day.)

(3) "Structural irresponsibility." The leaders of the political order take advantage of a structural weakness in all Democratic societies. Unable to depend on strong political parties, political leaders face the people alone and vulnerable, clothing

themselves in symbolism and wishes. Their promises of benefits become a special form of bribery endemic to democracy.

(4) "An ambitious adversarial class." The number of persons grows who see an expanded government, empires to conquer, personal security, wealth to accumulate, and personal power to acquire. Moreover, these growing numbers are increasingly led by an intelligent, able, persistent, and ambitious elite strong enough to rival the business elite in brains and purpose and power. In order to grow wealthy and powerful in a welfare democracy two roads now exist where only a short time ago only one did. The single road used to live through the private sector. Now a highroad has been opened through the public sector.

(5) "The declining status of aristocracy." The leaders of the moral-cultural sector have long suffered under the market system of democratic capitalism from a profound loss of status. By contrast, the dominant class within Democratic capitalism has been the commercial class. The standards of the market are only rarely the standards of artistic and intellectual excellence.

31

(6) "Envy." In Democratic capitalism, the resentments of the intellectuals are bound to fester. Monetary rewards for high intellectual and artistic talents, while in the vagaries of the market sometimes lavish, are more frequently less than rewards for top performers in corporate management, athletics, and entertainment. That fan dancers command moneys that many a scholar can scarcely dream of cries to heaven for justice. That a top talent in the field of corporate management commands a salary commensurate with that of a movie star rankles in the breasts of top academic and artistic talents.

(7) "Taste." The culture of democratic capitalism is loathed-- with perhaps the deepest loathing-- for its "bourgeois" and "philistine" tastes. Yugoslav socialist Bogdan Denitch adds, "There are two sides to this aversion. One is a predilection of socialist intellectuals toward the organized plans run by experts not too unlike themselves; the other is a notion that if customers of the lower orders are turned loose, they will not choose things that are good for them." (What hubris).

Michael Novak concludes that, "free to choose, a democratic people luxuriously manifests vulgarity. Plastic roses offend the sensitive. Rudeness and vulgarity in "shopping strips" assault the intellectuals. The tastes of ordinary citizens ... scrape against refined tastes like a fingernail across a backboard." (p. 35)

He continues, "Socialism is a neat solution to both grievances. It raises up a new elite to a position empowering it to impose a better way. Thus, its attack upon the aesthetics of democratic capitalism is an important step toward 'the reintegration of the political and the economic.' Such a 'reintegration' embodies a moral-cultural vision which is to be obligatory for all." (p. 35) The only problem being is that it creates more problems than it solves. It has never worked anywhere it has been tried.

Novak concludes that, "When the necessary work of society is so organized as to make the acquisition of wealth the chief criterion of success, it encourages a feverish scramble for money, and a false respect for the victors of the struggle, which is as fatal in its moral consequences as any other form of idolatry." (p.35,36)

In "Religion and Rise of Capitalism[10]", R. H. Tawney discerned as the dominant spiritual theme in Democratic capitalism the vulgar itch of acquisitiveness. Max Weber described capitalism as an "iron cage whose bureaucratic steel would crush the human spirit". Paul Tillich, a towering theologian, describes Democratic capitalism as "demonic".

Despite the vast influx of women in the workforce the median American family with two wage earners earned less real income in 1989 than a single income family did 20 years earlier. While wages have fallen the number of hours of work has risen. According to a Harris poll in 1973 the average American Adult had 26 hours of leisure time a week. But now has only 16 hours. I started my industrial career in 1956 married in 1960 and my wife never had to work. Today my children and grandchildren work from morning till night. They are never away from their cell phones and are constantly texting. The biblical story about the tower of Babel foreshadowed the world we live in. If you call it living.

---

[10] Religion and Rise of Capitalism by R. H. Tawney

Michael Novak concludes "in good faith who can be by conviction and by willingness to commit one's life to its defense, a democratic capitalist? Those who would do so are everywhere embarrassed by the lack of an intellectual tradition that will nourish them; or a theory that would satisfy them. A description of the world of their actual experience which is recognizably true".

Novak observes that many scholars have missed the fact that capitalism-the economic system-is embedded in a pluralistic structure in which it is designed to be checked by a political system and a moral cultural system. Democratic capitalism is not a free enterprise system although it cannot thrive apart from the moral culture that nourishes the virtues and values on which its existence depends. It cannot thrive apart from a democratic polity committed on the one hand to limited government, and on the other hand, the many legitimate activities without which a prosperous and favorable economy is impossible.

He concludes that under the government of the very homogeneous and doctrinaire majority Democratic government might be as oppressive as the worst dictatorship. "A true 'dictatorship of the proletariat' even if democratic in form, if it undertook centrally to direct the economic system, would probably destroy personal freedom as completely as any autocracy has ever done."

And so, it has. The last eight years of Obama's rule have been devastating! Debt has soared, black on black crime is greater than ever, entitlement has become the law of the land and almost 50% of our workforce is unemployed. Black Lives Matter, but not to blacks. The Chicago Mafia, in which I would include George Soros, Saul Alinsky, Rahm Emanuel, Hillary Clinton, Jesse Jackson and Al Sharpton, now run the country and our twits applaud.

There is no justification for the belief that so long as power is conferred by democratic procedure it cannot be arbitrary. Novak observes that if democracy resolves on a test which necessarily involves the use of power which cannot be guided by fixed rules it must become arbitrary power.

The June 2011 issue of Commentary Magazine correctly illustrates the dangers resulting from an out-of-control democracy. The author of "Why Corporations Love Regulation[11]", William Voegeli states, "To regulate means to 'make regular,' and the use of the word ought to connote practices that conform to clear, comprehensible, and predictable government standards. What we get instead are 'rules' that are complex and often indecipherable... Even worse than being complex, many regulatory 'rules' are utterly malleable and endlessly negotiable."

The Dodd/Frank bill in my opinion is one of the best examples of how government bureaucrats can engender tyrannical governance. The way I interpret their bill is that it enables government legislators to do whatever they want, however they want, to whomever they want. Voegeli continues to say, "In 'Power Without Responsibility' David Schoenbrod writes that because America has 'never dealt with the modern world' through a legislature that legislates rather than outsources its authority and duties to bureaucrats, we inhabit a regime that

---

[11] Why Corporations Love Regulation by William Voegeli

'reduces our participation in lawmaking, our understanding of how government works, and our power to hold legislators to account when the government fails to provide timely, balanced resolutions of regulatory disputes.'" Concern for equal opportunity is consistent with incentives and equality. Concern for equal results is not.

Among the unintended consequences of the pursuit of the equality of results is a heightening of sullenness and resentment. A society which judges less on the dynamism of opportunities, liberties, and mobilities and more upon the equal allocation of its benefits, feeds the fires of envy that it is presumably intended to quiet. In his 1944 masterpiece "The Road to Serfdom[12]" Frederick Hayek wrote that "in freedom crushing totalitarian societies the worst get on top". (And so, they have)

"To be a useful assistant in the running of a totalitarian state it is not enough that a man should be prepared to accept specious justification of vile deeds, he must himself be prepared actively

---

[12] The Road to Serfdom by Frederick Hayek

to break every moral rule he has ever known if this seems necessary to achieve the end set for him. Since it is the supreme leader (Obama) who alone determines the ends, his instruments must have no moral convictions of their own."

And so, they do not! Hillary Clinton and Tim Kaine are the worst of the bad and their election would have paved the path to a totalitarian America embracing the worst of political ideologies. We would no longer be the land of the free and the home of the brave. We would have been enslaved by entitlement related to your vote. Some of my most intelligent friends do not agree with them and more than 70% of my fellow Jews concur. They are wrong!

My professional career began as a roustabout in Smackover, Arkansas and took me around the world to some places which had never even seen a white person. I saw firsthand how totalitarian states had disenfranchised their citizens and confiscated their wealth. Mr. Putin nationalized the entire industrial state of Russia and put it in control of a handful of dutiful servants. Overnight a nation's infrastructure had been confiscated and its citizens enslaved. The same thing happened in Cuba. Castro took over with the support of many industrialists and overnight their businesses were confiscated and became the property of the state. The same thing has happened in North Korea and throughout the Arab world. Saudi Arabia did nothing to develop their oil resource for which they got paid the weight of their leader in gold. Then, they nationalized Shell, Esso Mobile, Chevron, BP, Texaco, Gulf, Standard Oil, known as "the seven sisters" and have held us hostage since then.

Mostly American technology developed all Arab oil resources. Mostly American dollars enabled the recovery of the free world after World War II. Mostly American military has protected the rest of the world from the tyranny of communism and socialism and mostly at our own expense.

It is time for America to regain its moral leadership and for the world to recognize its importance in defeating Islamic fundamentalists, defending against totalitarian domination and maintaining freedom. Otherwise, a return to the dark ages seems inevitable.

A coalition between Iran, Iraq, Libya, Syria, Saudi Arabia, Russia, China, Pakistan and most of South America seems to me inevitable if we don't return to the America we once were. Completely surrounded by our enemies and lead by un-American ideologues, I see a bleak future.

Donald Trump appears to me to be our last great hope for a return to greatness. Frankly I wouldn't do business with him, but his record was pretty much an open book. He is simply a hard business man who surrounded himself with very competent people. That is exactly what we need today to turn this train around.

From my Jewish perspective, a return to our Jewish roots would bring Catholics back to the Jewish Jesus and return God to a much more significant role in mending our fall from grace. The Bar Ilan teachings began with the codification of the Bible, Torah, Mishna and Talmud. From about the year 500 A.D. every generation of rabbis has pondered the meaning of that code handed down from God to Moses at Sinai. Since then we have been on "the critical path" to peace and the messianic age.

From the "Big Bang" 13.7 billion years ago to the messianic age a little over 200 years from now God has given us the wisdom to interpret his message using everything there is to know about everything knowable in order to implement the thousand years of peace expected then.

The final link in the critical path is to codify the Bar Ilan papers into an IBM "Watson" type computer, impanel a 72 person Sanhedrin to pose the questions and interpret the answers so desperately needed in our now misguided world.

ON THAT DAY, THE LORD WILL BE ONE AND HIS NAME ONE

This is what concerns me the most! In all my years, I have never been so depressed about the future especially for the future of my grandchildren. A good friend recently told me that her son has decided not to bring children into such a world. So much for "Be Fruitful and Multiply".

"The founders of Democratic capitalism intended to give greater scope to manufacturing and commerce than had been obtained under any previous form of political economy. They wished to build a center of power to rival the power of the state, they separated the economy from the state not only to unleash the power of individual imagination and initiative but also to limit the state from within and to check it from without. They did not fear unrestrained economic power as much as they feared political tyranny! Hayek got it right again.

It is the structure of business activities and the intentions of businessmen that are favorable to rule by law. They deliver the habits of regularity and moderation, to a healthy realism and to demonstrated social progress. It is in the interests of businessmen to defend and to enlarge the virtues on which liberty and progress depend.

What we were seeing was the attempt to impose equality of outcomes, which changes the focus of economic activity from production to distribution. This is a perversion to treat modern economic conceptions in such a way as to no longer reward results, except to the very few. It has reduced savings, investment and productivity. It necessarily results in a society more static than a free society. Concern for equal opportunity is consistent with incentives and inequalities, concerns for equal results are not. The latter must produce a zero-sum game. If rewards are by allocation, all but the privileged few will be living in dependency.

The system of Democratic Capitalism believing itself to be the natural system of liberty; is the system which so far in history is best designed to meet the premises of original sin. It is designed against tyranny. Its chief aim is to fragment, to check power, not to repress sin. Within it, every human vice flourishes.

Entrepreneurs from around the world flock to it and teach it new cultural specialties of vice as well as virtue, of indelicacy as well as delicacy. Our public immoralities are manifested in massage parlors, pornography shops, pickpockets, winos, prostitutes, pushers, poker chambers or group sex-you name it. Democratic capitalism tolerates it and someone makes a living from it.

And I thought that Elvis Presley with his vulgar dancing was the beginning of the end of America. The fact is a free society can tolerate the public display of vice because it has confidence in the basic decency of human beings, even under the burden of sin.

Our political system, for more than 200 years, has rewarded intelligence and hard work; in many cases, disproportionately, because of recent changes in our tax laws. These made stock options so lucrative with many executives earning up to 1000 times more than entry-level wages, even after firing thousands of workers. When I worked for Shell Oil Company our president made $250,000 a year and no one felt that he was overpaid or that they were not paid enough.

IQ matters and it is genetic. Money is not the motivator top management and the Board of Directors would have you believe. The stock option should be repealed and employee pay should be increased. When employees are paid fairly and managed effectively, everyone wins. Peter Drucker is a good reference for what our models should be.

The great libertarian fear, as I understand it, is that by combining roles the Constitution, separated and eviscerating its checks and balances in favor of giving administrators broad powers to seek their own solutions, the regulatory state we are now in can engender tyrannical governance, which we now have, by giving administrators broad powers to seek their own solutions. We have created a democracy ending tyranny.

I believe that by centrally directing our government from the top down without effective balance has resulted in the worst dictatorship in our country's history. Our founding fathers never intended for the executive branch to have the ability to ignore the will of our legislators. They did not fear unrestrained economic power as much as they feared political tyranny. Frederick Hayek makes this compelling argument in his book "The Road to Serfdom".

So now we are faced with historically unattractive choices. A crude and blunt, but successful businessman who selected an outstanding vice presidential running mate, versus a lying scoundrel who knows how to turn on a smile and charm when it suits her purpose and otherwise accept bribes from sources who are not our friends. But worse, she selected the worst possible person to become our vice president.

Should they win, our country will be run by the Chicago Mafia reflecting the views of George Soros, Saul Alinsky, Rahm Emanuel, Jesse Jackson and other left wing ideologues. The voter rolls enhanced by un-American immigrants will assure their continued reelection. Once done, it's over! (Trump won! We are safe!)

My career was spent working with the likes of many of Trump's supporters. The roustabouts and roughnecks I worked with could tear down a drilling rig, move it a mile away and have it running that night. When included in the planning, they can make almost anything work. While I don't personally like Trump's business practices, I do admire his ability to get things done. Further, I trust him to do what he says he's going to do and that is consistent with the best interests of our country.

I expect him to move our embassy to Jerusalem, the capital of Israel. I expect him to strengthen our military and take a stand against rising worldwide anti-Semitism, which is as great today as ever in history.

I believe kicking the UN out of the US is long overdue.

Arrogance, as reflected by Hillary and her running mate, is not only the monopoly of the rich and privileged. The concept of "entitlement" as espoused by Black Lives Matter leaves many of its followers to play victim and justify idleness, despondency and lack of responsibility. 99% of black voters voted for Obama thereby validating their prejudices. Even though he promised everything to everyone, he has produced little of consequence for anyone.

After his election, I had a letter published in the Austin Daily paper saying how proud I was to be an American that we had finally overturned the last remaining prejudice. I had torn up my McCain/Palin signs and was now an Obama Man. The very next day he changed my mind when he said now "we have to consolidate our base". Little did I know he intended to do that by allowing massive immigration of mostly Islamic believers.

He received 77% of the Jewish vote and in the last election received 74%. In this past election, Hillary received 70% of the Jewish vote. I don't get it. His actions on the world stage are anti-Israel and threatening to its very survival. His actions at the UN have consolidated its historic anti-Semitism and threatened unjustified boycotts related to Israel. His refusal to recognize Judaism's 3000 year claim to the nation of Israel, as bequeathed by God, attests to his ignorance of Israel's role on the path to peace. It undermines his validity as a Christian.

As well, his unwillingness to recognize the universal tendency of Islam leading to conflict, as is self-evident, leads me to suspect his motives. I wonder whose side he and the democrats are really on. I know it's not mine!

Even when it comes to alternate energy sources the present administration seems blind to the opportunities in our own backyard. Lawrenceville Plasma Physics is within five years of producing a 5-kW reactor capable of supplying sufficient energy to power 5000 homes for five years at a cost one 10th the price of coal. This can be accomplished without pollution or radiation risks with reactors transportable by truck. See the discussion "Fusion for Peace" later in this book.

This success will reflect a paradigm shift in the world's energy production and could eliminate atmospheric pollution from coal plants. Four of the world's top physicists visited their plant and saw no technical barriers to success. (I am an investor and a member of their board of advisors.) These reactors will be readily transportable anywhere in the world and would enable the drilling of water wells in the middle of the desert and the production of sweet water thereby.

According to our Jewish tradition, "the righteous beholding this, will rejoice, the upright will be glad, the pious will celebrate with song, evil will be silenced and all wickedness will disappear like smoke, when you remove the tyranny of arrogance from the earth."

We can bring that time when truth without dogma is seen by each of us through our own eyes in peace and without fear of the other. For that to happen we must defeat evil, seek justice, love mercy and work for peace. "The audacity of hope" will be achieved. We will turn swords into plowshares, spears into pruning hooks and peace will prevail.

ON THAT DAY, THE LORD SHALL BE ONE AND HIS NAME ONE

In order to fully appreciate how to stay on the critical path, Judaism must be seen as an evolving religious civilization predicated on the belief that the Lord our God is truth, as handed down from God to Moses at Sinai. 600,000 Jews and a similar number of non-Jews heard that message which has been studied continuously since then and finally codified in the Bible, Torah, Mishnah, Talmud, Zohar, Kabbalah and hundreds of other sources over more than 500 years and continuing even today.

It is the religion of Jesus, the foundation of Christianity and the guide to the future. Until that happens, we are destined to repeat the past and we are well on the road to doing so. The wisdom of the Bible reflects the collective mind of man; its proper interpretation requires some knowledge of everything there is to know about everything knowable. Otherwise, each field of knowledge has its own vision of truth, which requires every field of knowledge for understanding. There is one fundamental criterion, however, which requires that you be able to seek your truth without fear or threat from the other, no matter how outrageous or unreasonable or unbelievable. You were created with free will, including both good and evil. Your route is yours to choose even if it leads to teaching hate, raising children to become bombs and dancing in the streets when they kill innocent people.

Fortunately, others are biblically inspired to kill you for doing so and I hope they succeed, because good and evil cannot coexist in a free world. Mankind cannot see God's face or even understand his plan in a "world lit by fire". Our nation, under God, has been destined to lead the war against evil throughout the world. It cannot be won without us and it requires the cooperation of all free nations to support its cause and fund its progress. Our enemies are clearly evident but unspoken of by our leaders, who, for whatever motives, ignore the self-evident.

President elect Trump is changing that, and our young men and women who still volunteer for our Armed Forces get it, as well as those of us steeped in the wisdom that God gave to us. Sweet talking and smiles do not reflect the strength required to defeat Islamic terrorism, we believe that the defeat of evil is required for truth to prevail. Here's why!

CHAPTER 3

The Religion of Biblical Israel

It is time to pray! We must return to those religious roots which made this country great and from which Christianity evolved. "From the Big Bang to the Messianic Age" evidence supports that we are here by design. The rest of the story explains why.

The following discussion should help to make the case for the above scenario. It is based upon one of the six books referenced earlier encompassing everything there is to know about everything knowable.

AMERICA'S PROPHET
By Bruce Feiler

From the overleaf of his book: "The Exodus story is America's story. Moses is our real founding father[13]." The pilgrims quoted his story. Franklin and Jefferson proposed he appear on the US seal. Washington and Lincoln were called his incarnations. The Statue of Liberty and Superman were molded in his image.

Martin Luther King Jr. invoked him the night before he was murdered, Ronald Reagan and Barack Obama cited him as inspiration. For 400 years one figure inspired more Americans than any other. His name is Moses.

In his groundbreaking book, New York Times' best-selling author Bruce Feiler travels through touchstones in American history and traces the biblical prophets' influence from the Mayflower through today. He visits the island where the pilgrims spent their first Sabbath, climbs the hotel where the Liberty Bell

---

[13] The Exodus story is America's story. Moses is our real founding father by Bruce Feiler

was described with a quote from Moses, retraces the Underground Railroad where "Go down Moses" was the national anthem of slaves and dons the robe Charlton Heston wore in the 10 Commandments,

"Even a cursory review of American history indicates that Moses has emboldened leaders of all stripes," Feiler writes, "patriot and loyalist, slave and master, Jew and Christian. Could the persistence of his story serve as a reminder of our shared national values? Could he serve as a unifying force in a dis-unifying time? If Moses could split the Red Sea could he un-split America?

One part adventure story, one part literary detective story, one part exploration of faith in contemporary life, America's Prophet takes readers to the landmarks of America's narratives, from Selma, the silver screen, to the Oval Office, to understand how Moses has shaped the nation's character.

Meticulously researched and highly readable, America's Prophet is a thrilling, original work of history that will forever change how we view America, our faith and our future. In view of the recent ADL (Anti-Defamation League) report that anti-

Semitism is now greater than any other time in our nation's history the following selected quotes should help restore our faith.

"In coming weeks, I found a similar story over and over again: Columbus comparing himself to Moses when he sailed in 1492; George Whitfield quoting Moses as he traveled the colonies in the 1730s forging the great awakening; Thomas Paine in common sense comparing King George to the Pharaoh; Benjamin Franklin, Thomas Jefferson and John Adams in the summer of 1776 proposing that Moses be on the seal of the United States; and the references didn't stop. Harriet Tubman adopting Moses' name on the Underground Railroad; Abraham Lincoln being eulogized as Moses' incarnation; The Statue of Liberty being molded in Moses' honor; Woodrow Wilson, Franklin Roosevelt, and Lyndon Johnson tapping into Moses during wartime; Cecil B DeMille recasting Moses as a hero for the Cold War; Martin Luther King Jr. likening himself to Moses on the night before he was killed.

"For 400 years, one figure stands out as the surprising symbol of America. One person has inspired more Americans than any other. One man is America's strong founding father. His name is Moses." (pg. 4)

A few other quotes will help to explain why I am still puzzled about our nation's continued ambivalence regarding Israel as the homeland for the Jews.

Feiler quoted Jonathan Sacks the chief Rabbi of Britain who said, "The Hebrew Bible has been a radical political document testifying to the right of prophets to criticize kings, the inalienable dignity of the human person, and a clear sense of the moral limits of power." (pg. 22)

"The Puritans saw themselves as a chosen people being oppressed by a great Imperial force. Also, Jews had been kicked out of Britain by then, so in the absence of real Jews (it's possible for everyone to be Jewish) you can hijack their ideology, lock, stock, and barrel; which is essentially what they did." (pg. 30)

"As the Continental Congress gathered in Philadelphia in 1776 comparisons with the Exodus filled the air. From politicians to preachers, pamphlets to pulpits, many of the rhetorical high points of the year likened the colonists to the Israelites fleeing Egypt. Thomas Paine invoked the analogy in "Common Sense,[14]" the best-selling book of the year; Samuel Sherwood made it the centerpiece of the year's second-best selling publication, "The Church's Flight into the Wilderness." And on the afternoon of July 4, after passing the Declaration of Independence, Continental Congress asked John Adams, Thomas Jefferson, and Benjamin Franklin to come up with a public face of the new United States. They chose Moses." (pgs. 35-36)

"John Adams wrote that he always considered the settlement of America" the opening of a grand scene and design in Providence for the illumination of the ignorant and the emancipation of mankind all over the earth." (pg. 60)

"Since the Exodus, freedom has always spoken with a Hebrew accent". Since 1776 freedom is also spoken with an American accent in many places and has been visualized with the Liberty Bell. The union of the Exodus in 1776 in the form of the old

---

[14] Common Sense by Thomas Paine

Statehouse Bell is a celebration of the idea that human beings can imagine a better life for themselves." (pg. 71)

"The persistence of Mosaic rhetoric in the first decade of the United States testifies to the enduring elasticity of the Exodus as a trope in American identity. The fact that so many who invoked the story were members of the elite shows that reverence for Hebrew Scripture ran through even the highest segments of society and was not merely for rallying illiterate masses. All ten colleges founded on American soil before the revolution offered instruction in Hebrew. The Seal of Yale depicts an open Bible with the inscription "Light and Truth" in Hebrew. The Seals of Dartmouth and Columbia include Hebrew as well. The Harvard commencement included a Hebrew oration every year until 1817. Even in the face of the Enlightenment, the Hebrew Scriptures have stubbornly maintained their grip on the American mind. And Moses maintained his status as the Bible's chief ambassador to the United States." (pg. 95)

How ironic and disheartening it is, that today these very institutions which embodied the best of Jewish tradition have become leaders against the state of Israel and sponsor movements that today would have them divest their investments in Israel which benefit all of humanity. Israel is a "light unto the nations" and could lead the Middle East forward, but for the "teaching of hate". The "eggheads" supporting this ideology remind me of those other "eggheads" who would have us believe there is no God! If you continue reading after this point you will come to believe there is a God who provided us with a plan which should become the Critical Path.

The extent to which that case is made, reflects the degree that America without its Jews or Judaism would have no special status in God's view. I firmly believe that most Americans still share that belief and hold the expectation that God's will, will prevail.

Feiler's description of the Exodus story and how it resounded with African-Americans is particularly enlightening. It reflected the history surrounding my own pride in my country when Obama was elected president. My letter was published the day after the election in the Austin newspaper. We had broken the final barrier! I was now an Obama man. That lasted one day; for, the next day Obama declared we had to unite our base. He had received 99% of the black vote and 77% of the Jewish vote. He renewed the prejudice we had long fought and put us back on the road to disrespect and distrust.

We are now as divided as ever and "Black Lives Matter" has now become the mantra and the banner carried by Sharpton and Jackson and championed by those who would undermine what in fact is best about our country. Entitlement has taken the place of opportunity in the pursuit of happiness and it won't work! Neither will outrageous executive pay or lifetime election to public office.

I remember how proud I was when I voted for Johnson and Humphrey and their "Great Society" program. Then I watched Jackson, Mississippi, which had already integrated five grades in school without problem, go from segregated to integrated and then back to segregated, when forced bussing was required by the government. All this in less than five years convinced me that the Democrat ideal was not real. I have voted Republican since.

A few statistics about crime in the United States in 2013 as published by the FBI shed some light on why our problems are getting worse not better under the current leadership. Regarding murders as reported in the uniform crime reports Expanded Homicide Data Table 6 Murders:

3005 Whites were murdered by 2509 whites and 409 blacks: 2491 Blacks were murdered by 189 whites and 2245 blacks. Proving that Black lives may matter, but not to Blacks! Their movement defies reason and denies truth. Considering that Blacks represent less than 13% of the total population, their movement is built on a lie promoted by charlatans.

Returning to Feiler, he cited the story about John Parker, a Black preacher who lived by the tenet that "freedom is the right to be free and then the obligation to accept responsibility. If you don't understand that then ugly stuff happens and when you do understand that you are prepared to meet the obligations straight on." (pg. 132) Too bad we have no black leaders like him today.

Regarding the matter of religion, in early America Feiler says," Almost all Americans say they believe in God, 93% of American homes have at least one Bible and a third of the country believes the Bible is literally true. But few know more than its basic outlines. Half of Americans can't name the first book of the Bible and only 20% can name a single prophet. Gallup calls the United States a nation of biblical illiterates". (pg. 276)

We have lost our religious underpinnings and we have lost our compass. Abortion on demand, same-sex marriage, sex change operations, and transgender bathrooms influences as well how we view the poor and helping those in need.

My thanks go to Mr. Feiler for providing such fundamental insights into the Jewish influence on America. It is the land of the free and the home of the brave. We must all strive to keep it that way even while it is slipping away. A return to our Jewish roots is essential to restoring the hope that is America!

CONSTANTINE'S SWORD
THE CHURCH AND THE JEWS

According to the overleaf, "in a bold and moving book that is sure to spark heated debate, the columnist and cultural critic James Carroll maps the profoundly troubling 2000-year course of the Church's battle against Judaism and faces the crisis of faith it has provoked in his own life as a Catholic. More than a chronical of religion, this dark history is a central tragedy of Western civilization, its fault-lines reaching deep into our culture.

The Church's failure to protest the Holocaust-- the infamous 'silence' of Pius XII-is only part of the story: the death camps, Carroll shows, are the culmination of a long, entrenched tradition of anti-Judaism. From Gospel accounts of the death of Jesus on the cross to Constantine's transformation of the cross into a sword, to the rise of blood libels, scapegoating, and modern anti-Semitism, Carroll reconstructs the dramatic story of the Church's conflict, not only with the Jews but with itself. Yet in tracing the arc of this narrative, he implicitly affirms that it did not necessarily have to be so. There were roads not taken, heroes forgotten; new roads can be taken yet. Demanding that the Church finally face this past in full, Carroll[15] calls for a fundamental rethinking of the deepest questions of Christian faith. Only then can Christians, Jews, and all who carry the burden of this history begin to forge a new future.

Drawing on his well-known talents as a storyteller and memoirist, and weaving historical research to an intensely personal examination of conscience, Carroll has created a work of singular power and urgency. 'Constantine's Sword' is a brave and affecting reckoning with difficult truths that will touch every reader."

Garry Wills said, "This searingly honest book is Augustinian in the way Carroll searches his own soul, going down through layer after layer of instilled Catholic attitudes that demean Jews. We who had the same Catholic training badly need this book, to cleanse our souls, to make us all ask for forgiveness".

---

[15] Constantine's Sword by James Carroll

Bishop Christopher Stendhal the former Dean of Harvard Divinity School describes it as "a deeply religious book written in levels of understanding and with clarity and insights rarely- if ever-reached in the telling of this painful story".

Eugene Kennedy, author of "My Brother Joseph" says James Carroll's "Constantine's Sword" is an astonishing work of historical research that sweeps you up in the scenes of revelation that open, one upon the other, to explore the Church's role in anti-Semitism, a tale that has been told, at best, by halves before this. To read this book is a thrilling experience. It reveals unhappy truths about Catholicism in a profoundly Catholic Way. Carroll is a man who loves his faith but loves truth, too. He tells a story that every Christian must read and every Catholic must sense as an expression of a new consciousness of what it means to be a Christian Catholic."

But unfortunately, the most recent study by the ADL shows anti-Semitism to be more prevalent today than ever in history. Obviously, the authority of facts completely and accurately presented, even those endorsed by the Church itself, prove ineffective in preventing the present Pope from praising Abbas as a man of peace and describing the mountains of Judea and Samaria as the homeland for the Palestinians.

There are thirty-two paperclips in my copy of Mr. Carroll's book and I urge those of you who wish to understand history and its adverse impact on the Jews to read it. It's silly of me, however, to believe that another book will make any difference whatsoever, but like Mr. Carroll I am compelled to write it. By way of background it is useful to know that around the time of Constantine there were about 5,000,000 Jews in the world with a population of about 190,000,000 people. Today there are about 14,000,000 Jews in the world with a population of 6,000,000,000. What happened to about 157 million Jews is best understood by "In Hoc Signo Vinces" ("In This Sign Conquer").

Mr. Carroll explains this by the fact the "Jews accounted for 10% of the total population of the Roman Empire by that ratio if other facts have not intervened there would be 200 million Jews in the world today instead of something like 13 million". As a Catholic, he was asked by Pope John Paul II about the lack of progress in purging anti-Judaism from Catholic teachings. His opinion is that contemporary Catholic views are defensive and self-exonerating. It was Carroll's opinion that Nostra Aetate read like a post-show or attempt to disassociate the church of the diabolical effects of its own teaching, without really addressing the problem of that teaching. (pg. 43).

This inadequate review does not begin to emphasize the importance of this work in explaining the role of the church in contemporary history. You have to read it to know what it says. But what it meant was clearly described in the national bestseller discussed next.

"A World Lit by Fire[16]" by William Manchester accurately describes the horrors committed in the name of Christ under that sign, during the middle ages encompassing the Crusades. As discussed later, only an authentic return to its Jewish roots will redeem the Church from its mistaken path. Manchester helps to understand the medieval mind and the Renaissance as ugly as they were. His sources are complete and authentically described in the 267 books he referenced.

---

[16] A World Lit by Fire by William Manchester

The story bridges the time from Constantine's Sword "In Hoc Signo Vinces" (In This Sign Conquer) 316 AD until 1536 AD. Its effects still linger and worldwide anti-Semitism is greater today than ever in history proving that history is a poor teacher or that humanity is unteachable.

The portrait which emerges is a mélange of incessant warfare, corruption, lawlessness, obsession with strange myths, and an almost impenetrable mindlessness, this is reflected by St. Bernard of Clairvaux (1093-1153) who declared that the pursuit of knowledge unless sanctified by a holy mission was a pagan act and therefore vile. (pg. 9)

The Fifth Lateran Council[17] (1512-1517) reaffirmed that "outside the church there is no salvation. (pg. 20). Catholicism has thus found its greatest strength in total resistance to change and turning a blind eye to evil. Thomas Henry Huxley scored the church as "the one great spiritual organization which is able to

---

[17] The Fifth Lateran Council[17] (1512-1517)

resist and must, as a matter of life and death, the progress of science and modern civilization." (pg. 117).

The present Pope, in praising Abbas and recognizing the mountains of Judea and Samaria as the homeland of the Palestinians, shows the church has not learned much and offers little hope in achieving peace. According to a most important prayer in our upcoming high holy day observance "the righteous upholding this will rejoice, the upright will be glad, the pious will celebrate with song, evil will be silenced and all wickedness will disappear like smoke, when you remove the tyranny of arrogance from the earth. This could happen if the Catholic church would lead the way!

Paganism in the Bible – Exodus to Exile[18]
The history of biblical Israel describes a 700-year struggle between paganism and monotheism, culminating in the destruction of the Temple and the Babylonian exile, after which, paganism ceased.

---

[18] Paganism in the Bible – Exodus to Exile by Mordecai Kaplan

Kaufman suggests that paganism was not that firmly entrenched, and that the people believe the Temple destruction and exile was a result of the sins of pagan practices which they then stopped. The nearly 500 verses in the Tanakh citing these practices suggest they were too prevalent to be easily forsaken. Michael Fishbane attributes a major part in the epochal transformation of ancient Israel into ancient Judaism to the scribes. By education and love of God, paganism and immorality were overcome, an important lesson for then and now!

Mordecai Kaplan, the founder of Reconstructionist Judaism, defines Judaism as "an evolving religious civilization dedicated to changing what is to what ought to be". I agree! This description is clearly evident from a study of Tanakh theology covering the period between the Exodus 1280 B.C.E. and the exile 586 B.C.E. somewhat startling to the novice student is the struggle with paganism, which seems to have dominated this 700-year period. It was referenced in almost 500 verses in 27 of the 39 books of the Bible.

These verses include warnings against our punishment for various pagan practices a few examples of which follow. Worshiping no God's, other gods and idols, (Exodus 32:1, 32:4, 32:8), building altars and planting groves. (Deuteronomy 4:16-19 23, 25, 28); following the doings of Egypt and Canaan Leviticus 18:3; Moloch worship (Leviticus 18:21, 20:2-6); committing adultery, worshiping Baal and intermarriage (Numbers 25:1,2,3,6) Deuteronomy 4:3, 7:3, Joshua 23:12); abominations, passing through the fire, divination (Deuteronomy 18:9-12, backsliding, rebelling, and being stiff-necked.

As Kaufman notes in The Religion of Israel, page 141, the heyday of Judean idolatry was the reign of Manasseh (the North Korean leader of his day.) Kaufman describes him as the Jezebel of the South, whose acts appear to have aroused opposition which he suppressed with much bloodshed. Scripture describes the fall of Judah not to the sins of its last kings but the sins of Manasseh. (That's great, blame the kid!)

The bulk of the nation believed that the destruction of the Temple was the work of YHWH, hence there was no escape from the conclusion that they must mend their ways. Foremost among their sins was a provocation of YHWH with no god's. Only a thorough extirpation of those idols could assuage His anger. In this way, the great shock of the destruction of the Temple allowed the people to accept the final cultic consequence of monotheism and to leave idolatry forever.

Prior to the Babylonian exile Israel was only free of pagan practices during the time of Joshua and his generation. The book of Judges describes repeated backslidings resulting in the children of Israel doing evil in the sight of the Lord. True repentance and avoidance of pagan practices can apparently avert the evil decree and yet only a few years later, the children of Israel sinned in the sight of the Lord and the Lord delivered them into the hands of the Philistines for 40 years.

But even the kings made little difference, as is described in the books of Kings, Chronicles and Prophets. Kaufman suggests the nature of the popular idolatry as being a vulgar superstition that some of the monotheistic peoples practice to this day. He could have been referring to almost any modern fundamentalist religion, which tends to see a direct link between sin and punishment and describes ritual as more important than deeds.

Kaufman goes on to suggest that in pagan views, sin and punishment are by nature interrelated as cause-and-effect.... Evil causes misfortune to a man or his descendants; goodness purifies his soul.

Ultimately the Torah and prophecy recognize a primeval moral law obligatory upon all nations. Religion conceives of all as an expression of the will of God, his absolute command. What is, has been created by the goodness of God. This goodness has been revealed to man and man has been commanded to realize it in his own life. Man, was created here, into a world of moral goodness that ought to be, but he has the freedom to define God's will. This freedom is the root of sin and evil. The moral responsibility of man reaches its full justification in the idea of human freedom.

Thus, unlike paganism, man is a partner with God, made in his image and responsible for perfecting the world. Therefore, society has a duty to educate each member and look after his deeds... because society is under a covenant obligation to eradicate evil from its midst and cause justice to prevail. This moral conception, especially as it was expressed by the prophets, was beyond the scope of the ancient morality that had never heard of a claim upon society as a whole.

I believe that the message conveyed to the mass of Israel's people, after its documentation by the Scribes and after the Temple destruction resulted in the inner transformation referred to by Kaufman. To the scribes then, we owe our thanks for giving wisdom to the people to recognize the limitations of paganism and the moral and ethical role of Judaism. Through the efforts of the scribes the Bible became the book of the people. We became the people of the book and we pray that others will embrace its teachings without dogma getting in the way. Through reason, Judaism overcame the strong appeal of pagan practices. Through reason, we must help others do the same.

We must help Christians come back to their Jewish roots and see their religion through the eyes of Jesus.

AND ON THAT DAY THE LORD SHALL BE ONE AND HIS
NAME ONE

CHAPTER 4
Judaism versus Greek world myth

The different worldview presented by biblical and Greek myths: Western civilization would be far more just in its actions, and more messianic in its vision, if the Jewish biblical view had been more dominant in the evolution of Western society. The pervasive cynicism, helplessness, and hopelessness characterizing society today is reflective of a feeling of despair, alienation, and worthlessness that eats at the inner core of civilization even as it reaches its peak of military and cultural strength. Kaplan, Schwartz, "A Psychology of hope[19]".

Unfortunately, this Greek view seems to dominate world culture today. It is evidenced by the large number of murders, divorces, abortions, single-family homes, cynicism, disrespect for authority and each other, gratuitous violence, pornography, and gossip. Shows on television tear at the fabric of society, and in

---

[19] A Psychology of hope by Kaplan, Schwartz.

my opinion are manifestations of the "self-destruction which was a perverse motivating theme in Greek and Roman thought".

A clear understanding of the effects of Greek myths on Western thinking is evident from a careful study of Kaplan's book which emphasizes the question of suicide, as viewed primarily from the Greco-Roman perspective and to a lesser extent from the Christian perspective. The primary purpose of Kaplan's book is to demonstrate that the suicide preventing tendency emerges from the biblical covenantal perspective which contrasts with the suicide promoting tendency, which emerges from the classical Greek Roman narcissistic culture.

Numerous examples of suicide are described in the works of ancient biographers like Plutarch and Diogenes, Pythagoras, Socrates, Demosthenes, Mark Anthony, the statesman Seneca and his wife Paulina and many more. The futility of life in this world is revealed in Homer's world, where the warrior hero is the highest type of individual. (Think Drew Brees and the vast cast of football and basketball and other sports heroes.)

Although, always a nobleman and often descended from a God, the hero is fundamentally flawed and can never really win. Ultimately no amount of heroism is enough, no crown of glory is sufficient to bring satisfaction or add any value to his life. One can achieve success and recognition in the Homeric world only by means of heroism and competition. But the heroic life typically ends in miserable destruction, (or concussion).

How typical we are of Homer's world is described in an editorial by John Leo in the U.S. News & World Report of October 9, 1995[20]. "When twenty-three million isn't enough. Substitute the word money for heroism and you see the Greeks had it right. According to Leo, executive compensation showed that in the mid-1970s the United States at a 39 to 1 ratio between the corporations' most highly compensated executives and the average worker. His recent study of 292 CEOs, who have held their jobs for three years or more, show the ratio at 145 to one in 1992, 172 to one in 1993 and 187 to 1 just the following year. Now it is as much as 500 or even 1000 to one! These are combustible numbers! How long can any sane society tolerate

[20] Editorial by John Leo in the U.S. News & World Report of October 9, 1995

an ever-widening gap between the average worker and a new self-enriching class of ultra-wealthy managers?

Executive compensation is utterly out of control. These people never looked down to see what the average worker gets. They never look across to see how much less their counterparts in Europe and Japan get. They never look back to see how far they have come. They just look ahead at what other people are getting, and they want more. With an Internet, driven system such as this, does anyone think that reform will arrive on its own?

Dream on friend! In confirmation of this view, Seneca would suggest that "hope for the betterment of the human condition is false. Truth doesn't grow and neither does virtue. One must continue to try but not because there is any hope of success." The effect on the other end of the economic spectrum is seen in an editorial by Vincent D. Rougeau in the September 3, 1995[21] issue of the New York Times: "Societies ill-fated trade-off." In

---

[21] New York Times editorial by Vincent D. Rougeau, September 3, 1995

this editorial, Mr. Rougeau describes a marked shift in the contract and part-time work with a resultant loss in job security.

He suggests that this "is a prime example of what happens when an unrestrained free-market combines with profoundly egalitarian and individualistic culture like our own (read Greek). We are asked to believe that this new system of employee/employer relations is superior to the old because it offers freedom from the straitjacket of institutional conformity and capriciousness. "If you work hard and are the best at what you do the market will reward you with financial success. If you fail, there is no one to blame but yourself". Ayn Rand could not have said it better and neither of them could have said it worse.

We are all in this together and we are responsible for each other's welfare. As you will read later, Judaism describes an economic system that floats all boats. When you explore the sea of the Bible, the Torah and the Talmud as Jesus and his disciples taught, you will recognize an economic system and a code of personal relations underlying a just society.

Rougeau suggests that a culture that places little value on commitments between employers and employees will no doubt show similar disregard for commitments in other areas of social life. The American version of the free market can only flower in a society that exalts the autonomy of the individual, discounts natural human differences, and deemphasizes social and cultural connections that limit individual expression by community ties, personal responsibility and religion.

As a result, many economic decisions command a social and cultural price that we should never be willing to pay. Civilized living demands that we accept some restriction of our rights and freedoms and choices. These are a small price to pay to avoid the social anarchy and decay that lies at the end of the road we are now travelling.

The losers in the above scenario, like the characters in Greek tragedy, are trapped in no-win cyclical situations, not entirely of their own making. There is no way out of the cycle, nor is there much chance of seeing the alternatives clearly. Our Prophets, Jessie Jackson, Al Sharpton and Barak Obama, like Tiresias, speak in riddles that are meant to be misleading and unhelpful.

Oedipus has no saving answers to the riddle of the Sphinx, for there are none. There is neither hope nor prayer. The entire tragic context is a breeding ground for suicide or murder, helplessness and hopelessness, leading to record numbers of murders, abortions, fatherless children, and homeless mothers. Christianity, in my opinion, offers few answers because as Kaplan suggests, "it grew up within the Greco-Roman world, and its leaders were influenced by the Platonic ambivalence toward life and death and even by Stoic elevation of suicide and murder, disguised as a type of martyrdom. St. Paul's epistle to the Philippians is explicit in its almost Platonic praises of death over life.... It is easy to see an impatience and disdain for life in many New Testament passages and certainly the next world is considered preferable to this one.

It should be remembered that Christianity, in its first years, grew up among pagan cults. It soon absorbed strong elements of Greek thoughts as well, less intense eschatological excitement blended with the chronic depression of Greek philosophy. The New Testament focuses on the mystery and passion of the sacrificial death of Jesus as part of the divine plan to save mankind. "For God so loved the world that he gave his only begotten son that whoever believes in him should not perish, but have eternal life" (John 3:16). Love and sacrifice are closely intertwined throughout the New Testament.

According to William Nichols' "Christian anti-Semitism,[22]" "a history of hate" encompassed Greek ways of thinking in a Gentile church, which required a radical reinterpretation of writings, originally understood within the Jewish frame of thought. The center of this transformation was the New Greek doctrine of Christ, now thought of as fully divine! According to Nichols "the successful transformation of Christianity into Greek terms paved the way for the success that no form of Judaism could have enjoyed in the Roman world. But, in catering to these Greek and Roman views, Christianity became the romantic religion of which Leo Baeck said "lacks any strong ethical impulse, and will to conquer life ethically... It has an antipathy against any practical ideal which might dominate life demanding free, creative obedience....and showing a clearly determined way to the goals of action." Romanticism would like

---

[22] Christian anti-Semitism by William Nichols

to recover from purpose. All, all that legislates, all morality with its commandments is repugnant to it. It would rather stay outside the spirit of good and evil. The highest ideal may be anything at all, except the demands of ethical action. From all that urges and admonishes, the romantic turns away. He wants to dream, enjoy, and immerse himself, instead of clearing his way by striving and wrestling.

In this way, religion becomes redemption from the will, liberation from the deed. Leo Baeck said that the best commentary for Paul is found in Luther's words. "In all who have faith in Christ, reason shall be killed. Else faith does not govern them, for reason fights against faith." In the religion of Luther, Baeck concludes there was no inner compulsion to approach political and economic life in order to make it more ethical and to drive it forward. Its indifference toward any earthly upward tendency always made it easy for romantic religion to defend submission to every earthly yoke, even to preach it. Of the Pauline exhortation that every soul be subject unto the higher powers, one has always and with the greatest of ease gotten to the point of first tolerating every despotism and often soon consecrating it.

Thus, the ancient mystery religion got along very well with tyrants and these in turn were very well disposed toward it, because they could easily see that the devotee of supernatural events is an obedient subject on the earth below." Starting with Constantine, the Christians as the Greeks rendered unto Caesar. There frequently remains no significance whatever from anything further and especially ones' personal life's work. Instead of any positive judgment, there is merely hostile melancholy.

Also to Plato's thinking that the soul is a helpless prisoner chained hand and foot in the body compelled to view reality not directly but only through its prison bars and wallowing in utter ignorance. Thus, the real attainment of truth can come only in the higher world and can only perceive directly, without the interference of the body. This position does not necessarily lead to a direct call to suicide but it does foster the habit of thought, in which earthly life is but little and the philosopher is encouraged to believe that separation from earthly life is the only road to the ideal human existence.

We can conclude that the manifestations of the medieval Church reflect the powerful influence of Greek and Roman thought and that the Pauline dogma removes the very ground from under man's rights as a moral subject and as an ethical individual. The Pauline faith deprives ethics itself of its basis. Religion now becomes the contradiction of ethics each excludes the other in principle either faith or ethics.

According to Baeck[23], this indifference to the everyday life has led the church to being satisfied with itself. "It has been capable of beholding a great deal without being at all upset. The Christian religion, very much including Protestantism, has been able to maintain silence about so much, that it is difficult to say what has been more pernicious in the course of time: The intolerance which committed the wrongs or the indifference which beheld them unperturbed.

The Holocaust of 6 million Jews in Nazi ruled Europe was the greatest outpouring of evil in history!

---

[23] This People Israel by Leo Baeck

This could never have happened in a world governed by the Jewish beliefs of Jesus, his disciples and the followers of Judaism ever since. In contrast to the Greek and Christian worldview the ancient Hebraic writings condemn suicide and approaches duty and freedom in vastly different and more realistic terms. We Jews are created in the image of God and we are an evolving religious civilization committed to changing what is to what ought to be. Our mission is to seek justice, love, mercy, and to walk humbly with our God.

Our foundation is laid on the pillars of truth, justice, love and mercy all of which must be encompassed for God's word to prevail. In order to accomplish this requires a startling idea, a state-of-the-art message among the Christian scholars writing about Christian anti-Semitism as a basis for the Holocaust. He suggests a return to the God of the biblical revelation of Jesus.

By moving in this authentically theological direction it becomes once more possible to recognize radical evil and the ultimate triumph of God over it. Such a theology would now involve a rethinking of Christianity from its roots. It would be necessary to revise Christian theology, not only in the light of historical discoveries, but also even more in the light of the biblical faith in the one God who revealed himself through the events of Israel's history. Who gave the Torah to Moses at Mount Sinai, who has not abandoned his covenant with his original people and who continues to rule the world as evidenced by everything known to man?

Only along this path can Christians begin to meet the agonizing problems of anti-Jewish Christianity once more encountering the Jewish Jesus. Our Christian brothers must choose between the Gentile religion of Paul and the Jewish religion of Jesus and his disciples.

ON THAT DAY THE LORD SHALL BE ONE AND HIS NAME ONE

An authentic move of Christianity back to its Jewish roots would also require a religious view of creation and a view of God as an intelligent designer.

CHAPTER 5

An Intelligent Designer

It has been evident from Einstein's time and confirmed by all modern science, genetics, astrology, chemistry, physics, and biology. On March 9, 2004 astronomers at the Space Telescope Institute unveiled the deepest portrait of the visible universe ever achieved. Called the Hubble Ultra-Deep Field, the 275-hour exposure reveals the most remote galaxies yet seen, more than 13 billion light years away. The picture was published in the book entitled "The Universe and Beyond" and it is a most incredible survey of the known universe. You can probably Google the picture which describe a patch of sky smaller than a pinhead held at arm's length.

To observe the entire sky at this resolution with the Hubble space telescope would require almost 1,000,000 years of uninterrupted observing. You do not have to take my word for it, you can see it for yourself. If you don't believe it after that, nothing I can say will change your mind. Our galaxy came along about 4.5 billion years later and our planet is uniquely situated for life. From my DNA analysis, it has been conclusively determined that single cell of life began only about 550 million years ago and God and the Angels have only enjoyed our pitiful efforts to understand for the last 10,000 years.

God boosted our ability to understand when he handed down the Torah to Moses at Sinai about 3500 years ago. Now, we have the whole plan in place and if we bother to, we can learn whatever we need to learn about how to deal with each other and reach an age of peace, scheduled only about 225 years from now. For that to happen Christians must return to their Jewish roots. There just are not enough Jews left. We were 14 million, at the same time China had 14 million. Today there are 1.6 billion Chinese. If you have to ask what happened to the Jews, it was the Christians, the Poles and the Germans and all the rest who watched. It's now time to join us and take an active role in bringing Christians back to their Jewish roots to help in mending the world.

There are two traditional views that this the world existed before creation – as chaos—Tohu wa bohu, i.e. dark energy and dark matter. Supposedly, that constitutes 96% of the mass of the universe and is what remained when God withdrew in order for us to exist. According to Dr. Howard Smith renowned astrophysicist 360,000 years elapsed after the Big Bang and before temperatures cooled enough for matter forming the universe to begin to condense.

In the beginning was silence, an Aleph, the first letter of the Hebrew alphabet. Moses on Mount Sinai is pictured as asking to understand creation the way God understands-- three times he is asked and three times he is told – ALEPH – the silence which encompasses all.

There is no way that Moses would have understood anyway. What would he have known about the Big Bang? The distribution of matter in space, the genome code or all the science, mathematics, chemistry, physics, and myriad of other disciplines required for understanding. So, God handed down the code at Mount Sinai and we have been deciphering it ever since.

It has required using everything known about everything knowable to properly interpret it. And it has been an ongoing process for more than 2500 years by Jews. Isaac Newton was a late comer and modern science began with the computer age in the 1920s.

We are now entering the most explosive age of learning approaching infinity. We are learning more than we know how to use and faster than we can use it. The" twit" has become the modern tower of Babel. Now everyone knows everything about everything there is to know. Or at least that's the great fallacy and threat for this know it all age

Everybody has an opinion and expresses it faster than most of us old guys can hear. We need to slow down and come back to our roots. Or we need to program IBM's Watson with all the writings from the Bar Ilan papers. Then impanel 70 experts from our various think tanks to pose the questions and interpret the answers. Now we are full circle back to the" Fractured Republic" and how to answer the questions posed therein.
Then we can elect Trump/Pence and feel confident that the program results will serve the needs of all Americans.

SUMMARY

Modern astrophysics posits that the universe, as we know it, approximately 13.7 billion years old, that all matter and energy were contained in a single point in space and for reasons unknown a "BIG Bang" occurred which led to the formation of all the galaxies, the stars and planets and moons that exist today. Billions and billions and billions of them. And still other hypotheses posit that we can perceive only about 4% of the solid matter that exists. The rest is dark matter, present and not accounted for. Whatever existed before the 'Big Bang' is a matter of speculation. With a degree of humility, scientists call everything before this moment, as well as the content of black holes—singularities-- meaning quite simply that our current laws of physics have no way of explaining our understanding of this.

There might be a parallel universe composed of antimatter or there may be many parallel universes of which we are totally unaware. There may have been a cycle of universes created and destroyed. String theory posits multiple dimensions which may have only mathematical existence. (Rather boring I believe). Current theory posits that approximately 4,000,000,000 years ago, our solar system was formed along with its planets, their moons and our Earth. So far along the way conditions developed that allowed for life forms. Simple organisms evolved into more complex plants and animals and about 500,000 years ago the first hominid creatures made their appearances and here we are today.

Scientific speculation itself has evolved over the centuries. But one thing is clear. Science is involved with how things have happened or may have happened. It is not concerned with why they happened or what it all means. And since people from time immemorial have been concerned with such questions, we must turn to other forms of human inquiry to approach them.

It is not that science or scientists view such as not capable of being elucidated by scientific testing in the scientific method. Einstein for example, might speculate that there is order rather than chaos because "God does not play dice with the universe." But that statement is a personal conviction incapable of being assessed by either science or mathematics. Indeed, there are times when personal conviction may interfere with scientific inquiry illustrated as by Einstein's struggle to accept quantum theory or the uncertainty principle. In our search for meaning, we must step out of the laboratory and find our own Bo-Bo tree under which we can ponder. But in our pondering, we must factor in the truths that science provides us with.

Medieval scholars reasoned that since the human drama was central to God's creation, the earth must be in the center of the solar system, and that since the circle was the most perfect geometrical configuration, the sun and the other planets must orbit around the earth in circular patterns. Such speculation proved to be scientifically inaccurate. The earth happens to revolve around the sun and in an elliptical orbit. Marxist theorists like Lysenko asserted that Lamarckian concepts of the inheritance of acquired characteristics right ideologically correct but of course they proved to be scientifically incorrect what all of this means in terms of research for philosophic and theological truth is another matter. In the face of scientific evidence, it is still possible for some to believe that the universe was created about 6000 years ago, but to do so is to declare that the accumulation of scientific insights is irrelevant. A science with no inquiry as to meaning or purpose leaves most people uneasy. A philosophy that takes no account of science may seem to most people out of touch with reality.

We now wander out of the laboratory into a realm where the search for meaning is but a small part. We may sit at the feet of the Socrates or Buddha wearing black, even as we may weigh their perceptive reasoning against our understanding of human nature and/or speculation on the mind of God.

The enlightenment believed that our speculation about meaning could be based on our understanding of the world of nature-- that standards of morality could be derived from a study of the natural world and primitive mankind. Such beliefs were naïve at best, geese and swans and wolves may be monogamous, the ducks, sea lions, and deer are not. The highly intelligent dolphins and porpoises are promiscuous and at times practice gang rape. Our nearest relative in the world, the chimpanzee, at times collected large groups and go out on raids, attack and kill neighboring clans, and cannibalize their victims. Marauding lions and bears commit infanticides to bring females into heat. A weasel in a henhouse will kill for pleasure.

Among seals, walruses and deer, males rule the roost. In elephants, lemurs, muskrats, moles, and rats, the females reign.

Even in supposedly noble savages, we can find every behavior imaginable. Some tribes require the killing of an enemy to prove one's manhood and the flesh of the vanquished may be eaten. Among tribes descending from the same ancestors in New Guinea we find extreme aggressiveness and extreme pacifism. Marriage in one tribe is a kind of warfare and the roles of men and women are clearly distinguishable. Children are handled roughly with almost no signs of affection. In the other tribe, marriage is an extension of friendship; male and female roles overlap and children are treasured and showered with affection.

If we look at so-called civilized people we find the same range of behaviors. The Greeks and Romans practiced infanticide and the status of women was clearly inferior. They both practiced slavery. Roman entertainment included watching wild beasts kill hapless human victims. Roman forms of execution were planned to prolong the agony. Roman legions practiced genocide on conquered rebellious peoples. During the Crusades. Christian hoards tortured and murdered countless numbers of nonbelievers and heretics in Europe and the Middle East. Invading Muslim armies were equally savage in dealing with infidels. In Africa, they kidnapped women and children and use them as sex slaves. Arabs and Christians both practiced slavery and considered their captives subhuman. Religious wars between rival sects left countless victims throughout the centuries.

What are we to conclude from all this? That morality, such as it is, is not natural to either man or beast. It is a human development. Moral codes cannot be derived by observing the behavior of creatures in the natural world. In most cases, moral codes have been derived from religious systems of belief-- which is not to say that all religious people behave morally and that all belief systems lead to what we might call moral behavior-- or that atheists cannot develop moral values.

But the contrast between the purely scientific notion of creation and, for example, the biblical version, is clear. No moral imperatives can be derived from the Big Bang theory. Science is ultimately morally neutral—value free. Man, appears on the scene as the product of evolution. In the biblical version of creation man is created to embody moral values and any individual or group that fails to uphold the explicitly enunciated values is held accountable for its shortcomings. There will come a time when all mankind will be judged.

We can access and focus on the biblical account, not because it is the only account that focuses on the purpose of creation, but because it is most familiar to Western readers. It can illustrate how philosophers and theologians go about making sense of our existence. But even here we have conflicting interpretations of the most basic kind.

Does the text suggest that God created the universe ex-nihilo or that the universe existed as primal chaos that God structured? Whichever approach we take whether we believe creation took only seven 24 hour days or seven periods of ages, we get a clear statement: God looked at what he had made or structured and found that it was good. That is a value statement that leads to other dramatic statements which are obvious or self-evident. Hindu and Buddhist philosophers speculate that the world of perception is an illusion. That enlightenment consists of merging with the immaterial reality that lies beyond perception.

Manicheism posits that physical creation was the product of an evil deity with equal power of the good that created the spirit. Other systems of belief posit that creation was incidental or accidental and that the gods had no regard for what they had created-- or for mankind in particular.

But according to the Bible, creation is seen as good. There was a plan to creation and to history. Apple trees produce apples, not potatoes. Dogs produce puppies, not tadpoles. Human beings come in two forms, male and female, so that they can be fruitful and multiply and spread out to fill the Earth. They are given dominion and guardianship over the rest of creation. These are all value statements. The ancient rabbis went further and asked why an all perfect, self-sufficient God needed to create the world in general and human beings in particular – creatures who would question the meaning of their own existence and the existence of their creators and could behave in ways that were not congruent with the divine will.

The sages created stories to explain such mysteries. One such story has God talking to his heavenly host about the creation of humanity. The scenario is based on the text which states, "Let us create man in our image." This suggests that there were other beings whom God was addressing. If there were no people, there had to be others with whom God could reason, i.e. Creatures with some level of discernment and insight. They voiced their opinion that God should not create humanity because people will disappoint him by their behavior. God acknowledges that the road will be bumpy, but he asserts that mankind are capable of learning moral values, that the experiment will be worth it since mankind was in fact, created.

One must assume that God's wisdom transcended that of the angels. That is because our moral purpose is to learn compassion. Biblical passages also assert that man was created in the image of God – all human beings-of all races ages and genders. As such, each human being is infinitely precious. "If you save one life you save a world". If you injure a person, kill someone's cattle, or damage property there is monetary compensation that is to be paid, but there are no monetary damages to be paid for the death of a person because a person's value cannot be calculated. It is beyond all monetary considerations. Even the condemned fellow cannot be left on the gallows to become food for scavengers. That would demean that individual and show disrespect for his creator.

This exposition is not meant to be a comprehensive study of biblical values but a comparison of biblical and other cultural norms. It suggests, however, that a moral dimension is central to our questioning of the meaning of existence. One could bring such a perspective to all human activity, for example, in business. A greater profit if it comes at the expense of those who produce the goods or services or to those who purchase those goods and services can be judged on moral as well in simple economic terms. In the early 20th century, for example, companies produced defective toxic products that were useless or deleterious. They kept their workers in unhealthy conditions and at levels far below the poverty level. They made huge profits, but over the years such practices were judged to be immoral and would change to benefit workers and consumers alike.

Collective-bargaining, unemployment compensation, social security, and workmen compensation were all based on moral considerations. We would say that doing the right thing may turn out to be more profitable. A quick view of companies that didn't follow such practices will show they paid heavily for their lapses. General Motors paid heavily for failing to replace an inexpensive defective part. Volkswagen's cost for faking emission standards ran into the billions. BP's offshore blowout resulted in the careless death of 11 employees because BP was in a hurry to vacate the drilling rig in order to save money! Worse of all, none of those executives responsible for the decisions were convicted or ever charged with manslaughter. Only a low-level engineer was tried for not properly spacing a centralizer. Ludicrous!

The Bible indicates that the first plan for human creation did not work out too well. Adam and Eve were not content to remain in childlike innocence in the Garden of Eden. Their descendants were deemed so evil that God destroyed all but one family. Beginning anew, the descendants of Noah didn't fare much better. So, God limited the age of people, eventually deciding to work with a single couple and their descendants, Abraham and Sarah, two people who were imperfect, but at least have the awareness of the importance of morality, as defined by the contract with God. And so, the era of myth ended and the era of history began. The biblical concept of history is that it is linear and purposeful and that God is a caring divinity that at appropriate moments intervenes to move history in his desired path. He uses imperfect humans to fill his ultimate purpose. There is, in fact, a purpose to history – where finally, all mankind that follow a moral course will return to innocence. Those who don't follow the course will pay the price.

We get one shot at life, or do we? The Genome code suggests otherwise, as our ancestry has been traced back thousands of years, even to the single cell from which all life evolved. Biblical writing introduced the concept of ultimate justice, tempered with mercy and grace. There will be some kind of afterlife where this judgment will take place. The nations that follow the model plan will be rewarded collectively. Individuals will be similarly rewarded or punished.

Eastern philosophies can say that history is being cyclical. We get reborn innumerable times until we achieve a level of enlightenment that allows us to escape the prison of material existence and join the ultimate unity of creation. In its purest form, Eastern philosophy pictures no personal creator-- no divine intercession-no God of justice, mercy, or grace or love. We get exactly what we deserve (our Karma).

Rebirth is the price we'd pay for not having achieved enlightenment. In traditional African culture, despite all the hardships life entails, life is considered to be such a blessing. Unlike the Greek tragedy, having done something so terrible that one does not deserve to be reborn is the worst outcome.

But whatever the story, one theme seems to be almost universal: moral behaviors in some sense have consequences of major importance. The stories may differ, but the moral qualities in which they are based are frequently deciding. In the Judeo-Christian tradition, these moral principles are codified. They are implicit in the behavior of the patriarchs and matriarchs. They become explicit in the handing down of the law on Mt Sinai. You don't have to speculate. Don't murder. Don't commit adultery, and so on. After the "10 Commandments" (in Hebrew the "10 statements,") the bare-bones commandments can be fleshed out. Jewish tradition identified 613 of them. Even among Jewish scholars, there was some disagreement as to which ones made the list. The early church eliminated the dietary restrictions and the need for circumcision and changed the day the Sabbath should be celebrated.

But, there was still a Sabbath and later on, some food restrictions. (No meat for example during Lent and in some cases on every Friday). Catholics did allow for statuary of Jesus and Saints, but they did not condone the worship of idols. The prohibitions in Jewish law are sometimes not understood when compared to the public at large. (No ostrich meat, no shrimp, and no oysters!)

The principles of interpersonal relations do make clear sense. Treat the stranger like a member of the family. Save the corner of your fields for widows and orphans. Reliable weights and measures. Don't usurp your neighbor's property by surreptitiously moving boundary markers, etc. If one follows the logic of the Bible, not only is following the moral precepts intrinsically good and beneficial to society, but is pleasing to the creator, who in his wisdom established those principles in the first place.

More than half the laws of the Hebrew Bible relate to temple sacrifice. Once the second Temple was destroyed by the Romans in 70 CE and it was clear that it would not be rebuilt in the foreseeable future, the religion had to find equivalent sets of practices to replace those Temple sacrifices. A group of sages gathered in the small town of Yavneh to accomplish that task. They instituted a prayer service to replace the morning, afternoon, and evening sacrifices and an additional service for the Sabbath and holiday sacrifices. Prayer services, study of the original texts and the performance of acts of lovingkindness, were deemed appropriate substitutions for the sacrifice. By then, discussion and elucidation and interpretation of the texts was a normal feature of Jewish life. Initial discussions were preserved orally-- but eventually they were written down in the Mishnah and in greater elaboration in the Talmud (codified by the fifth century CE). But the process continues to this day! What should be done if the blue dye that was used to color one thread on each corner of the prayer shawl was no longer available or became prohibitively expensive?

Other matters of contemporary importance relate to a mother's health during pregnancy. If prenatal testing determined that the fetus had inherited disease that was 100% diagnosable and 100% fatal, abortion is allowed at any time. Otherwise, abortion is not allowed after the first trimester except to save the life of the mother.

A compendium of such discussions and decisions are to be found in the Bar Ilan papers dating back to 500 CE, the discussions are considered to be Oral Torah and divinely inspired. The later prophets debated as to whether the choseness of the Jews by God was a unique gift or could be applied to other nations (and religions) as well. The sages made a distinction between pagans (idol worshipers and monotheists by Christians and Muslims. There was some speculation as to whether the concept of Trinity disqualified Christianity as a monotheist religion, but the dominant opinion considered Christianity as a form of monotheism. In areas controlled by Christians or Muslims, it was not politic to apply polemics to dominant entities that held the power of life and death over their Jewish minorities. But the later prophets had already developed the concept of multiple choices.

The God of the universe allowed each nation to develop its own contract with the divine, with its own system of moral principles and its own ritual and practice. Even paganism was valued as a first step in man's journey toward a belief in the one true God. The mandate to wipeout the life of the seven tribes in the holy land was promulgated with the idea that they can influence the Hebrews to adopt abhorrent practices like child sacrifice and orgiastic rituals and the worship of strange gods. The idea, also, was that the land itself was sacred and would not tolerate such practices by non-Jews and Jews alike. On one occasion, only six tribes were mentioned. The sages postulated that by accepting exile, they were granted land near Carthage (in present-day Libya to live out their lives peacefully. Only one people was rejected totally, the Amalekites, for being totally devoid of any concept of morality. They preyed on the weak and the elderly on the edge of the Jewish camp. They demonstrated the principles of nature (of carnivores) and thereby placed themselves outside the human community.

ISIS is the present embodiment of who Amalek represents: teaching hate, raising children to become bombs and dancing in the street when they kill innocent men women and children. Beheading unarmed prisoners and gratuitous acts of terror and destruction explain why King Saul lost his crown for his failing to kill Amalek. He killed every other man, woman, and child but left

Amalek and his descendants are who we must deal with today. The weapons and technology are ours to use but the will is weak. That may be a fundamental flaw of Christian societies governed by the principles of love and mercy. Islam is governed by the principles of justice and truth. Only Israel is governed by all four foundations of truth, justice, love and mercy as instructed by God. The Islamic truth is based on the Koran as taught by Mohammed an itinerant and illiterate peasant who warred against his brother, his family, his cousins, his community and all he perceived to be his enemy. None trusted the other!

If all nations have their own contracts with God, and the minimal test for virtue of non-Jews was adherence to the Seven Noachide laws. Traditionally enumerated, they are:
1. Do not deny God.
2. Do not blaspheme God.
3. Do not murder.
4. Do not engage in illicit sexual relations.
5. Do not steal.
6. Do not eat from a live animal.

7. Establish courts/legal system to ensure obedience to the law.

There was little reason for proselytizing among the nations. There were periods of proselytizing limited practically by Christian and Muslim bans on such activity (under penalty of death) but there were also little efforts to incorporate and modify pagan practices into Judaism. The Catholic Church was more accommodating, redefining pagan gods as Christian sites and reshaping the celebration of the ritual, celebration of the death, and resurrection of pagan gods into the Communion services during the mass. The birth of Jesus was moved to December to replace a pagan celebration (along with the Christmas tree) and the prolifically fecund rabbit became the Easter Bunny.

The irony for the Jews was that religions did aggressively pursue conversion of nonbelievers and persecuted those that did not comply – including the Jews. Constantine made Christianity the official state religion of the Holy Roman Empire in the fourth century. In a move to create unity in the Empire, the Council is convenient to establish the doctrine of the church. All other beliefs were declared to be heretical, and heresy was now punishable by death. Jews were suspect because they refuse to accept Jesus as their Messiah and the gospel as the new revelation. Paul, in his mission to convert the Gentiles, declared that Jewish law had been superseded. Jesus was the last one obligated to fulfill the law. Belief and faith in him now constitute the only road to salvation. He declared that a belief in Jewish law would obviate the significance of Christ's death and resurrection. The destruction of the second Temple in 70 CE was seen as a sign that God himself had removed the mode of atonement for sin from the Jews. The mantel of chosen has now passed to Christianity and the Christian Scriptures were now labeled the New Testament. There developed a contempt for Judaism and its followers that is expressed over the centuries and persecution, the isolation of Jews in ghettos, economic deprivation, expulsions and programs-- leading finally to the Holocaust.

In the Muslim world, Jews (and Christians) could be tolerated at times with second-class status, punctuated at times by persecution, exile and massacres. Islam ultimately sells itself as the only true religion and those who did not accept the Quran as the final and most perfect revelation of God and Mohammed is the greatest of prophets were at the very least regarded as dhimmi—nonbelievers-and at worst as infidels one can connect the situation of Jews in Europe to the atrocities perpetrated in the Crusades; to the mass slaughter during the plague years; to the Inquisition, the Chmielnicki Uprising, the state organized programs in Eastern Europe, the wave of anti-Semitism in the 19th century Germany and France; and as epitomized by the response to the Dreyfus affair. Hertzel's Zionism was born out of the fear of radical anti-Semitism which was confirmed 35 years after his death by the Third Reich.

It continues in the UN General Assembly: Israel is singled out as a pariah nation. Seventy-seven of the motions to censor nations for their actions are focused on Israel while the most frequent abuses of other nations are ignored. There has been only one motion censoring the Palestinians! The most vocal diatribes are issued by nations with far more egregious violations of human rights. Meanwhile Arabs glorified terrorist martyrs, subsidizing families and pledging to destroy Israel and slaughter its people. As one Jihadist put it, there will be peace in the Middle East only when Israel lies in pieces. (Maybe it's time to move the United Nations out of America.)

It has been documented as recently as two years ago by the ADL confirming that anti-Semitism is greater today than ever in history. Jews are leaving Europe by the tens of thousands! And anti-Semitism on our campuses is fueled by the false and infamous rhetoric about the "Palestinians". That is a fiction created by Yasser Arafat, and is a lie.

In recent years, there have been efforts to develop economic theories with a moral basis that is nonsectarian and non-dogmatic in character. The gap between rich and poor has widened in both the developed and in third world nations. Tax shelters and stock options have rewarded the upper echelons of business. Outsourcing to the Third World has made economic. Development in the US more precarious, one can hardly find a garment or an electronic device that is made in America. Greed, lack of oversight, and regulators with questionable economic policies have devastated the scene – producing an economic slump second only to the Great Depression of 1929.

Frederick A. Hayek in his book "The Road to Serfdom" focuses on the dangers of trusting government to decide how best to regulate the economy. In so doing, government has in fact turned out to be as oppressive as any autocracy.

So now we have completed the circle from start to finish and back again. Only a bona fide return to our Jewish roots will restore the integrity of our nation and the principles upon which it was founded. It is time for us to pledge allegiance, and our loyalty, to the last bastion of freedom on Earth. We should move our Embassy to Jerusalem, proving our faith in God and our Jewish brothers!

CHAPTER 6

FROM THE BIG BANG TO THE MESSIANIC AGE

Critical Path Planning is a useful tool for properly allocating human resources in pursuit of a commercial plan. It is commonly used, for example, before bidding on an offshore lease which might require five or more years and thousands of man-hours before installing the first platform offshore. This is particularly useful information when deciding on how much to bid for a prospective lease.

It is also a useful concept in attempting to understand God's plan for us mortals which God might have conceived in order for us to reach the messianic age in the Jewish year 6000. or 2242AD by our calendar. In fewer than 226 years, we are supposed to begin 1000 years of peace.

The books previously mentioned will have a significant role, but the most important book was handed down by God to Moses on Mount Sinai a little over 3000 years ago. According to my

117

understanding of the Midrash; first, God met with the Angels slightly more than 13.7 billion years ago, to discuss his critical path plan for creating man in his image, with free will and the knowledge of good and evil.

The Angels were astonished. Everything was fine as it was. The Angels resisted, but God insisted, I am going to do it anyway! With the plan, I'm going to give them, mankind will learn how to turn swords into plowshares, feed the hungry and clothe the naked! With that, God began to withdraw from space thereby compressing the energy in the universe to a density where a massive explosion occurred: "A BIG Bang", causing super acceleration of the remaining space which is ongoing today.

(Author's note: This Midrash is my fanciful version of how things began. It is no more unlikely than the most fanciful version of our most famous physicists who do not believe in God. It is consistent with the view of Dr. Howard Smith, an Astrophysics Professor at Harvard University and author of "Let There Be Light". As well, he believes God may have created several similar worlds in order to bring ours to fruition.)

That burst of energy more than 13.7 billion years ago created trillions of stars and more than 100 billion galaxies before a single planet, circling an insignificant sun, burst forth 4.5 billion years ago with conditions ideal for life to begin unlike any other planet in the universe. Considering that only 4% of the mass of the universe is accounted for by the stars and planets we were lucky. The rest is "dark matter and or dark energy" still unknown to most.

The first single cell of life started 550 million years ago,. Continued evolution, now proven by the genome code, describes the genetic structure of all life forms, which resulted in humans first appearing about 500,000 years ago. Our progenitors were about 10,000 humans found in central Africa and are the ancestors from whom we have all evolved. As well the genome code establishes our bond with all other life and gives us reason to understand why "the lion might lie down with the lamb and a child might tread on the hole of the asp".

However, when Cain slew Abel, God realized that man must have access to the plan he prepared and he chose Abraham and Sarah and their children to begin its implementation. A most disagreeable, stiff-necked family of ne'er-do-wells you have ever encountered, but they were the most hospitable. Sarah was constantly feeding, housing, clothing strangers, even threatening ones who were so bad that they were later turned into pillars of salt!

After nearly starving in the desert, they ended up as slaves in Egypt for hundreds of years, and God realized that some adjustments needed to be made in the plan. He bombarded Pharaoh with ten plagues, the last causing the death of the Egyptians' firstborn, including the son of Pharaoh. Only then did Pharaoh "let my people go" but still chased after the Jews, only to be drowned along with his soldiers.

God was then with the Jews, Moses, Aaron and Miriam during their wanderings in the desert for some 40 years to purge that generation which had been slaves for so long. During those wanderings, God decided he had better hand down his plan and decided to do so at Mount Sinai and advised Moses of the same. There, a multitude of 600,000 Jews plus a similar number of pagans, all gathered to hear God's Word. Moses ascended the mount to hear God's message because the people, while hearing it, were frightened by the noise of thunder and flashes of lightning. Those followers waited 40 days and 40 nights, not knowing that Moses was chiseling the immortal words of the Torah in stone. Becoming impatient, they smelted a golden calf from the jewels worn by the women and then danced around it, mostly to give them something to do while they continued to wait for Moses to return.

God advised Moses of what was going on, and Moses became outraged! He broke those original tablets and encouraged God to destroy the people because they weren't going to be good. God said, "No I'm not going to do that. You're going to go back down and lead them to the Promised Land." Moses did so but because of some errors he made along the way God said that he could see the Promised Land but he wasn't going to be able to enter it. So, he passed the mantel of leadership to Joshua, who "fit the battle of Jericho and the walls came tumbling down" more than 3700 years ago.

Rabbi Akiva later sent 25,000 rabbinic students into the countryside to record the observations of every man woman and child who experienced Sinai and heard God's message. These rabbis wrote down every single observation, carefully edited those that were most appropriate, and finally codified them in what became the Torah, the Mishnah, the Talmud, and the Teachings. The latter are still ongoing and are encompassed in the Bar Ilan papers still being written from a traditional rabbinic perspective.

With those as a guide, Jews have always been in "the promised land" which was never claimed by any other people until 1967 when Arafat preposterously claimed Palestine as the homeland of the Arabs who did not even exist at the time the Jews conquered the land. That claim is but a manifestation of the war against the Jews, which has been ongoing since the death of Jesus, probably by crucifixion by the Romans.

Beginning with Constantine; who made the church built by the followers of Jesus, a tool of the state, Christianity became a messenger of death for its Jewish founders. Many Jews were attracted to the Galilean Jewishness of Jesus, but most never even heard of him. The Sanhedrin and the leaders of the temple cult did not resist when the Romans; threatened by increasing multitudes of Jews attracted to Jesus, had him crucified. Then

Paul, following the four apostles who knew Jesus personally, became the apostle to the non-Jews and he taught that if there is salvation through the LAW that Christ died in vain.

From that time forward "the teaching of contempt" as supported by Constantine ultimately led to the horrors of the Holocaust described in Leviticus 26:14-39 and Deuteronomy 28:15-68. Jews have lived through 2000 years of that terrible teaching including the Crusades, the Inquisition and the singular horror of the torture and then murder of 6 million Jews including 1.5 million children.

This would not have occurred if it had not been for the "Secret war against the Jews", assorted conspiracy between the Arabs, oil interests, the CIA and the State Departments of both England and America. We could save the monuments but not the Jews. Even after Kristallnacht, when Hitler clearly showed his intentions to kill the Jews, he offered them freedom at the Wannsee conference. Both England and America torpedoed that effort at its inception. Fewer than 400 were accepted by Puerto Rico (?). Millions could have been saved.

Today the UN embodies the very spirit of evil which distorts truth and vilifies the messengers of truth who would defeat tyrants and embrace humanity. This Orwellian charade is an affront to any who believe that teaching hate; raising children to become bombs, and dancing in the streets when they succeed in killing innocents, even their own is evil. It is following in the footsteps of Amalek and was foretold when King Saul lost his kingship because he left Amalek alive. So, we have been threatened and murdered repeatedly throughout history and threatened even today by ISIS.

Even though the Library of Congress is accessible in the most remote regions of the world in the language of choice we are no closer to peace than ever. Three trillion calculations per second are not fast enough to spread truth. What is worse is that ability is being squandered by greed self-aggrandizement and hubris.

CHAPTER 7

THE ARAB MAN

Today, the United Nations embodies the very spirit of evil which distorts truth and vilifies the messengers of truth who would defeat tyrants and embrace the quest for peace. This Orwellian charade is an affront to any who believe that "teaching hate, raising children to become bombs and dancing in the street when they succeed in killing innocents, even their own" is evil. It is not just their way of viewing the world. It is following in the footsteps of Amalek and it will lead to tyranny. No one will be free.

We must come to understand that evil is real; that it is the ongoing threat to civilized life. The story of "Amalek" is the story of tyranny. When Saul lost his kingdom for failure to slay Amalek and every man woman and child and all their cattle, God said there would always be Amaleks among us. And so there have been: Genghis Khan, Hitler, Mussolini, Tojo, Stalin, Mao, Pol Pot, to name a few and so there are Hussein, Ahmadinejad, Khomeini, Gadhafi and others yet.

125

The most dangerous are members of or supported by the Muslim Brotherhood. Their creed is described by The Imam the *Said* (Martyr), [Hassan al-Binna] who said:

Oh [Muslim] brothers, the nation that excels in the death industry, and knows how to die a noble [death], Allah grants it a precious life in this world and eternal bliss in the afterlife. The only weakness that shall humiliate us is the love of this world and hating death. Therefore, we have prepared your souls for great action, strive for death – and life will be given to you. Know that there is no escaping death, and it will happen only once, and if you carry it out [death] for the sake of Allah, there will be profit in this world and reward in the Afterlife, and nothing will harm you except what Allah has decreed [for] you... Work for an honorable death, you will be thus granted full happiness. May Allah provide us and you, the honor of achieving the Shahabad [Martyrdom] for Him.

The founder of the Muslim Brotherhood, Sayyid Qutb was described in "The Looming Tower" as being from a mud walled village in Upper Egypt. His writings had earned him the fury of King Farouk and his friends had moved him to Greely, Colorado in 1949. Here is where he developed his views of America as socially corrupt, before Elvis, Playboy, Penthouse and Hustler. In case any of you should believe there is room for moderation.

Compared with Jewish teachings involving tens of thousands of scholars over more then two thousand years, and ongoing today, as the foundation for peace; the Koran is the word of a Bedouin peasant evolving only according to the most radical edicts of self proclaimed prophets. The one will lead to an age of love and peace, the other to degradation and destruction. There is no room for negotiation, because Arab conflict-proneness precludes it.

Rafael Patai's "The Arab Mind,"[24] was described by the New Yorker as "a sympathetic, wide-ranging study" and yet Ibn Khaldun, whom Patai described as "undoubtedly the greatest historical genius of his time as well as the greatest ever produced by the Arabs," had this to say: "Places that succumb

---

[24] Patai, Rafael, "The Arab Mind," Scribners 1973

to the Arabs are quickly ruined. The reason for this is that [the Arabs] are a savage nation fully accustomed to savagery and the things that cause it. Savagery has become their character and nature. They enjoy it because it means freedom from authority and no subservience to leadership. Such a natural disposition is the negation and antithesis of civilization. The Arab can obtain authority only by making use of some religious coloring. Because of their savagery, the Arabs are the least willing of nations to subordinate themselves to each other, as they are rude, proud, ambitious and eager to be the leader". (Pg. 20) This from fellow Arabs.

Lest you think this only applies to Arabs, Khaldun's disciple Taqi al-Din Ahmad al-Maqrizi, the most eminent of Mamluk historians and himself an Egyptian, says about his countrymen, "The Egyptians' character is dominated by inconstancy, indecision, indolence, cowardice, despondency, avarice, impatience, disdain of study, fearfulness, jealousy, slander, falsehood, readiness to denounce others to the king … the vilest faults produced by the meanness of the soul". (Pg. 21)

I believe the book should have been entitled the Islamic Mind because it describes the much broader conflict including Persians, Egyptians, Turks, Arabs and Bedouins. According to Patai "all this is to be understood in terms of the people who have lost their way, whose heritage has proven unequal to modernity whose leaders have been dishonest, whose ideals have failed. In this aspect, the new Islamic upsurge is a force not to solve problems but to intoxicate those who cannot longer abide the failure to solve them." Conflict proneness "is in the Arab bloodstream." (Pg. 218) I strongly urge the reader, and especially our political leaders, to reference Patai's writing to more clearly understand the nature of our enemy and the most effective way to victory.

Per Wilfred Cantwell Smith, Arab and Egyptian societies have deteriorated to a point where violence is almost inevitable. So, now we witness a people who teach hate, raise their children to become bombs and dance in the street when they murder innocent civilians, even their own people. Flying planes into buildings, killing thousands, are the most telling measure of their place in humanity. Unless totally and hopelessly defeated, (Pg. 225) the worst is yet to come.

While our Saudi "friends" are considered more moderate, its strain of Sunni Islam, known as *Wahhabism,* is not. Per Osama bin-Laden, "Every Muslim from the moment he realizes the distinction in his heart, hates Americans, hates Jews and hates Christians. This is part of our belief and our religion."

Compare this with "seek justice, love mercy and walk humbly with your God, feed the hungry, clothe the naked and turn swords into plowshares," and the stark difference between a God-centered and a man-centered religion is seen as the difference between good and evil. Judaism evolved continuously from the time of Abraham until the codification of the Torah. This period of 3000 years involved thousands of scholars continuously devoted to interpreting God's message, their sole purpose being to achieve peace.

Table I provides a sampling of sources dealing with six subjects as described in four major books of Jewish teachings. It speaks for itself. How many Muslim Sources deal with the same subjects? Any?

	TORAH	TALMUD	MIDRASH RAHBASH	ZOHAR	TOTALS
TRUTH	111	464	201	353	1129
JUSTICE	59	211	360	110	740
MERCY	73	291	274	363	1001
PEACE	249	500	600	332	1681
LOVE	155	278	427	357	1217
JERUSALEM	667	1436	583	177	2863
	POSITIVE PRECEPTS				8631

And yet the recent uprising in the Arab, Egyptian, Persian worlds comprising Sunnis, Shiites, Hamas, Hezbollah, Palestinians, Muslim Brothers and others all hostile to each other and ungovernable by any, holds the promise for Muslims leading the world to peace. But only when and if they focus on their problems, without blaming Israel for their failures, will the road to peace and prosperity for all be open. Three hundred billion dollars per year of oil income flowing into the Muslim infrastructure could raise the living standards for the entire Middle East and afford opportunity for all to prosper, especially if they allowed Israeli ingenuity and capability to help their efforts.

It is ironic that, in a time when the library of Congress is accessible in the most remote regions of the world in the language of choice, we are no closer to peace than ever.

It is always easy for someone to say what people should or should not do. While I agree that it would be desirable for Muslims to accept Israel's ingenuity in assisting Islamic powers to grow and prosper with a better administration of their resources, I cannot perceive a path of understanding between our cultures. We are basically different people.

However, we are not different at our sources we are cousins. We may be of different culture but we are all children of the same God. In the case with the Arabs, we are children of the same father. Ishmael and Isaac were brothers and even though our understanding of God's persona may be vastly opposite one another, we would like to be at peace with them. While we strive to find and implement solutions to our differences, the aim remains the same – we endeavor to be at peace with them.

Despite the Arab Man's weakness and his nefarious character traits, ninety percent of them are fundamentally good people." But, they have been led by tyrants who have used their weaknesses as a weapon against themselves, as did fewer than three thousand Nazis. The madness that pervades the minds of these despots has shed the blood of many innocent lives – and that for centuries. Moreover, this incessant manipulation of the followers of Mohammed has transformed Islam of ancient times into the monster of today. The Arab Man's fatalistic mind has been his downfall.

"Here is what Pope John Paul II had to say about Muslims." in an excerpt from "Crossing the Threshold of Hope" (pg.93).

Whoever knows the old and New Testaments, and then reads the Koran, clearly sees the process by which it completely reduces Divine Revelation. It is impossible not to note the movement away from what God said about Himself, first in the Old Testament through the Prophets, and then finally in the New Testament through His Son. In Islam all the richness of God's self-revelation, which constitutes the heritage of the Old and New Testaments, has definitely been set aside.

Nevertheless, the religiosity of Muslims deserves respect. It is impossible not to admire, for example, their fidelity to prayer. The image of believers in Allah who, without caring about time or place, fall to their knees and immerse themselves in prayer, remains a model for all those who invoke the true God, in particular for those

Christians who, having deserted their magnificent cathedrals, pray only a little or not at all.

The following proposal describes what I believe could result in a paradigm shift. Resulting in the world's path to peace. Successful implementation would enable feeding the hungry and clothing the naked, worldwide. As well, coal powered plants could be replaced and uranium production could be banned.

As discussed later in "Fusion for Peace," this could also be a vehicle for fruitful and mutually beneficial cooperation with Iran.

CHAPTER 8

THE WEST BANK

The following two papers were prepared by a college junior during his year abroad in Israel. They were written in 1985 and are as important today as when they were written. Nothing has changed!

Is the Palestinian question the major obstacle to peace in the Middle East? In order to test this theory, one must first understand the history of the development of this region, the evolution of Arab and Israeli thought processes, the results of recent conflicts in the Middle East, and the projected results of establishing a Palestinian homeland in the "administered territories." Through a challenge of the centrality of the Palestinian Arab problem, this paper will determine the reasons for the public's perception of this problem as the most significant barrier to the Middle East peace.

Conflicts between Israel and the Arab states developed quite recently in history, after 1917, when the Balfour Declaration was presented to the British parliament. Arab nationalists asserted that the land of Palestine had already been promised to the Arabs in the negotiations of the McMahon Correspondence with Hussein ibn Ali, Sharif of Mecca. However, Winston Churchill as Colonial secretary referred to the correspondence and stated that his government regarded Palestine as excluded by these provisions. The Mandate system, created at the Treaty of Versailles after World War I, entrusting the land known as Palestine and Iraq to Great Britain, aimed at assisting local communities towards independence. Thus, Iraq became an independent state in 1932 and Transjordan in 1946. Syria and Lebanon, under French Mandate, became independent states in 1936 and 1941 respectively. In addition, Saudi Arabia and approximately fifteen other Arab states arose in

Middle Eastern territories. Recognizing that Palestine was the historic Land of Israel, it was not accepted that Palestine should be another Arab state simply because of 700,000 Arabs living in it. These Arabs were a tiny fraction of a community of many millions covering vast territories. But the Jewish National Home provisions of the British Mandate were then declared inapplicable to Transjordan and confined to Western Palestine, following anti-Jewish riots in 1920 and a crisis in Arab territorial dispute in 1921. This meant that nearly 70 percent of the Mandated area was closed to Jewish immigration. Further concessions to Arab opinion were reflected in the Churchill White Paper which limited Jewish immigration by economic capability, but this was toned down eight years later, enabling Palestine to absorb 80,000 Jews from Nazi Germany after 1933. Arab feelings of the Jewish immigrations were seen in violent outbursts of protest in 1929 and again in 1936 led by the Mufti of Jerusalem, extremist leader of the Palestinian Arabs. British troops were sent to Palestine with a royal commission, led by Lord Peel; that reported that the Jewish and Arab positions were too far apart to be joined in a single country and recommended the establishment of a small Jewish state, a larger Arab state, and a continued Mandate over Jerusalem. The Zionist leadership, however reluctant, was willing to accept these "Peel" proposals for discussion; however, the Palestinian Arab leaders rejected the proposals, demanding that all of western Palestine become another Arab State. At this time, Britain sought to keep Germany and Italy from winning over the Arab countries by issuing the White Paper of 1939, providing the establishment of an Arab state with a Jewish minority and limited Jewish immigration of 15,000 per year for five years. The desperation of German Jewish, even after the Holocaust, was ignored by the British, who detained boatloads of refugees in detention camps in Cyprus. The Zionists demanded a Jewish State and

Britain turned to the United Nations. The result was the UN Partition Plan of 1947, calling for separate Jewish and Arab states, with Jerusalem as an international zone. While the plan had serious shortcomings, such as indefensible frontiers, the Zionist movement accepted the proposal. The Palestinian Arabs prepared to destroy it by force.

The Israel Declaration of Independence included the following, adopted on 14 May 1948:

> We extend our hand to all neighboring states and their peoples in an offer of peace and good neighborliness, and appeal to them to establish bonds of cooperation and mutual help with the sovereign Jewish people settled in its own land. The State of Israel is prepared to do its share in a common effort for the advancement of the entire Middle East.

The next day, Egyptian, Syrian, Jordanian, and Iraqi forces converged upon Israel. After three weeks of intense fighting, a United Nations peace treaty was established, enforced after Arab refusal. This intent of the Arabs to destroy Israel creates a history of battle in recent Middle-East history from the 1956 Israel-Egyptian War, to the Six Day War of 1967, to the 1969-70 War of Attrition, and the Yom Kippur War of October 1973.

To understand the Arabs' extremist views on the destruction of the State of Israel, one must briefly understand the evolution of Arab thought. Since the time of the Pagan religions of the nomads, the Arab has seen no difference between political loyalty and religious belief. There exists no separability of church and state. Thus, a political war between the Arab states and Israel can be linked to a religious war between Islam and Judaism, justified by the Arab concept of Universal conquest by Islam of "dar el Harab," the world under war or under non-Islamic rule. In addition, it can be justified by the concept of Oriental Despotism, a western label for the Arab culture, outlining the need for inequality, of a strong centralized power dominating its subjects, and of a society based on the norm of warfare.

To understand the Israeli position, one has to only look back as far as Nazi Germany. With no place to go in Europe, and reluctance of the British to offer Palestine, Zionists accepted what they could. While the UN Partition Plan was far from what they wanted, the Jews accepted the proposals for discussion. The Armistice Demarcation Lines of 1949 were only a result of Arab attack on the new state. Likewise, the acquisition of the Sinai from Egypt and Judaea and Samaria from Jordan were a result of Arab offenses, not Israeli. Before the Six Day War on 26 May, 1967, Gamal Abd al-Nasser, President of Egypt proclaimed, "... we're ready to enter into war with Israel. It is not a separate action. The battle will be a general one and our basic objective will be to destroy Israel."

Having lost on the battlefield, how would the Arab States attempt to destroy the state of Israel? Perhaps they would use propaganda to influence the International community towards their cause. A possible explanation can be found by studying the Palestinian Arabs.

Who are the Palestinian Arabs? After the birth of the State of Israel, the Arab population of Palestine became split up, about 600,00 moving to Judea-Samaria, the Gaza strip, Transjordan, Lebanon and Syria, and about 160,000 staying in Israel and becoming its citizens. Judea-Samaria was annexed by Jordan, and Jordanian nationality, which has been retained under Israeli administration since 1967, was extended to the refugees. The Gaza Strip was occupied by Egypt until 1967, but Egypt did not extend nationality to its inhabitants, thus remaining   stateless   since

1948. In Syria and Lebanon, the Palestinian Arab refugees were also not given political nationality and remained stateless. Nearly four million Palestinian Arabs are now spread across the world, attracted by employment opportunities. Two-thirds of the total number live in Israel or Jordan, so they are not a "stateless people in exile." In fact, they already have a homeland in Jordan, which has a Palestinian-Arab majority. Sir Alec Kerkrade, Britain's East Bank representative asserted,

> [Jordan] intended to serve as a reserve of land for use in the resettlement of Arabs, once the National Home for the Jews in Palestine, which they pledged to support, became an accomplished fact. There was no intention at that stage of forming the territory east of the river Jordan into an independent Arab state.

Under the auspices of the Arab League, the Palestine Liberation Organization was formed in 1964. At first, it served as an instrument of Egyptian

143

policy, then Syrian. With the defeat of the Arab armies in 1967, the PLO became the self-appointed instrument of the struggle against Israel. The PLO claimed a national entity, assuming all the different groups of Palestinian Arabs form a single entity and national destiny, despite the fact that they have never said so. The organization became a terror organization, aiming to eliminate the State of Israel. In its "National Covenant," it outlines that the Arabs are entitled to self-determination and that the State of Israel has no right to exist, declaring the Mandate for Palestine null and void. With these proclamations as guidelines, it is clear to see the true motives behind the PLO. Looking back on history, independent statehood for the Palestinian Arabs was rejected in 1937 with the Peel report and again in the 1947 UN Partition Plan, because it would have meant Jewish independence as well.

If the major obstacle to peace in the middle East is not the Palestinian Arab problem, but rather the Arab refusal to accept the existence of a Jewish State, then why does the public's perception of the Middle East Situation reflect Israel's retreat to the pre-1967 Armistice Lines as the major obstacle. James Michener, historian and author, wrote:

> Following World War I, the countries of Europe absorbed a million, five hundred thousand refugees. Following World War II, the countries of Europe had to adjust to thirteen million refugees. Following the India-Pakistan War, the two sides absorbed upwards of fifteen million refugees. But in the wake of the Arab-Israel war, the Arab countries proved themselves totally incapable of absorbing a few hundred thousand refugees, for which they were themselves, largely to blame.

Why does the public perceive the conflict as the obligation of Israel? David

Sinofsky, in his article, "Balance and Responsibility in the Media," examined the New York Times' coverage of the Iran-Iraq War and the West Bank clashes. Despite the incredible number of people killed and money spent in a battle so close to Iran's major oil fields, the Iran-Iraq War was given almost no coverage; on the other hand, the West Bank clashes involved only limited property damage and eight deaths, but were relegated to front-page coverage. Sidorsky explains there is a belief in the media that "the conflict between Israel and the Arab states is the crucial factor for peace and stability in the Middle East," and that the "conflict between Israel and the Palestinian Arabs is the crucial factor for peace between Israel and the Arab states." Sidorsky's reasons for disproving these theories include the fact that the Arab states have fought twelve wars in recent history, including Syria and Jordan against the Palestinian Arabs. Phil Marfleet, in an article on Israeli propaganda, maintains that Israel is losing its credibility for the Western media. He showed the results of a poll that most Americans believe Israel should not have invaded Lebanon. Perhaps not, but the media might have altered the reporting of the war. In a review on the media in Lebanon, Joshua Muravchik, Strategic Studies Analyst, documents numerous cases of misleading or misinterpreted reporting, most notably the grossly exaggerated figures of 10,000 dead and 600,000 homeless reported by correspondents to newspapers, magazines and television broadcasts at the beginning of the war. When the correct figures were released, they were sometimes amended to the reports, but never with much clarity to the topic. Muravchik continues through sixty-five pages to present evidence of misreporting in Lebanon. The following gives a more clear-cut example. In its June 21 issue, Newsweek stated that "The Israeli Air Force and ground troop reduced Demur to rubble." Newsweek did not notice that the PLO had destroyed the bulk of Demur in 1976. A week later Newsweek published this account of the war:

> After the waves of terror bombing and indiscriminate shelling, no one could count the bodies buried in the rubble of Lebanon's coastal cities. Hundreds of thousands of refugees huddled on beaches and scavenged for food and water.

There was no "terror bombing" or "indiscriminate shelling" at this point in the war, he reports. Refugees, but not even hundreds of thousands of them, were not left on beaches, but returned to their homes, which were intact.

Biased reporting in the media can be seen outside the war in Lebanon as well. In "The Economist" of 28 March 1981, Jordan is given the status of "peacemaker" and King Hussein as 'one of the few Arab leaders of guys and stature." "Guts," they say, while the Jordanians say the only practical way forward is for the Palestinians to establish a state in West Bank and Gaza. Remember, they speak of a people with whom they went to war fifteen years ago. In another section of the article, "The Economist" states there are 10,000 Palestinians in the United States. Even the Palestine National Council admits there are over 100,000 Palestinians in the US. Could it be that the Palestinian lobby in the United States does not want its presence known?

While these cases of misreporting may shock the public, the censorship issue in Israel has been blown apart. "The Middle East" magazine reported in August 1982 that "Al-Fajr" weekly achieved only 40 per cent pass rate and that one feature writer submitted material for two months without a single piece passing censors. Further information on "Al-Fajr" from "Middle East International" reveals that the newspaper is the creation of a wealthy American entrepreneur of Palestinian-Arab descent, who one served three months in federal prison for trying to smuggle stolen equipment to the PLO. It reports that the paper has undercut its credibility. Once, when it reported that the Israeli military headquarters in Tyre had been accidentally bombed by Israel's Air Force, structural flaws caused the collapse.

For those who do not recognize the impact of the media or those who question Israeli censorship, Secretary of State, George Shultz said near the end of the siege of West Beirut, "The Symbol of the War is a baby with its arms shot off." Referring to a UPI photo captioned:

Nurse feeds a seven-month old baby who lost both arms and was severely burned late yesterday afternoon when an Israeli jet accidentally hit a Christian residential area in East Beirut during a raid on Palestinian positions to the West...

A few weeks later, Israel produced photos and affidavits proving, even to UPI's satisfaction, that a PLO shell, not an Israeli bomb, had caused the child's injuries, and further, the child had not lost his arms and his injuries were not severe. Imagine the impact that Shultz's statement had on public perception of the Middle East situation, and imagine what further impact it would have had on political relations had the mistake not been corrected.

It has been established that the crux of the middle east conflict is not the establishment of a Palestinian homeland in the "administered territories," but rather Arab refusal to accept the existence of a Jewish state in any part of what they consider the Islamic-Arab world. It is seen that the political, universal community news falsely portrayed the situation, due to misreporting and misinterpreting in the media. While striving for peace between Israel and the Arab states it is important to recognize propaganda and maintain objectivity in viewing the overall Middle East situation.

BIBLIOGRAPHY

1. Comay, Michael. <u>Zionism, Israel, and the Palestinian Arabs.</u> Keter Publishing House. Jerusalem. 1983.

2. "The Economist." <u>Steam from the Middle East's backburner</u> March 28, 1981. p.54

3. Friedman, Robert. <u>Arab paper talks to Israelis.</u> "Middle East International." April 15, 1983. p.15

4. Marfleet, Phil. <u>Israel's other war.</u> "The Middle East." August, 1982. p.12

5. Michener, James. <u>The Drifters</u>. Random House, Inc. USA, 1971. p.181

6. Muravchik, Joshua. <u>Misreporting Lebanon</u>. "Policy Review." Winter, 1983.

7. <u>The Palestine Liberation Organization: Liberation or Liquidation</u>. Israel Information Center, Jerusalem, 1979.

8. Rubenberg, Cheryl. <u>The PLO: Its Institutional Infrastructure</u>. Institute of Arab studies, Melmony, MA p.9

9. Sachar, Howard M. <u>A History of Israel, From the Rise of Zionism to Our Time</u>. Random House, New York, 1981.

10. Sidorsky, David. <u>Balance and Responsibility in the Media</u>. "The New York Times" on the Iran-Iraq war and the West Bank Clash, Midstream June/July 1982

11. Zion, Sidney. <u>The Palestine Problem: Its All in a Name.</u> "New York Magazine." March 13, 1978. P.43

It is important for the reader to realize that the situation has not changed what-so-ever since 1985. 800,000 Jews who were forcefully exiled from their homes and property, where their families had lived for hundreds of years, were mostly immediately resettled in Israel. The Arabs, who mostly left Israel against the advice of the Israeli government, and at the urging of the Arab nations, then at war with Israel, have been held in refugee camps ever since. The 1.4 million Arabs who elected to remain in Israel are prospering thereby.

The following paper describes the moral dilemma faced by Israel in their efforts to resolve the situation.

On Return of the West Bank: A Halakhic View

As greater concern is generated over the return of the West Bank, it is increasingly important to investigate not only the political implications of the transfer, but the Halakhic ones as well. Article A of "The Framework for Peace in the Middle East Agreed at Camp David" establishes the ground-work for the "administered territories:"

Egypt and Israel agree that, in order to ensure a peaceful and orderly transfer of authority, there should be some transitional arrangements for the West Bank and Gaza for a period not exceeding five years. In order to provide full autonomy to the inhabitants, under these arrangements the Israeli military government and its civilian administration will be withdrawn as soon as a self-governing authority has been freely elected by the inhabitants of these areas to replace the existing military government.[1]

Does Halakha agree with the signing of these provision on behalf of the Israeli government? Or do these provisions require the sale of parts of the Land of Israel from Jews to non-Jews, which is not permissible according to Halakha? Further, is the Israeli government permitted to instigate a war that would threaten its survival, by refusing to return the territories? Finally, do Jews not have the obligation to war with Israel's neighboring Arab states, in their ongoing war with Amalek? These questions must be examined before the Halakhic view on the West Bank can be realized. "And Abraham hearkened unto Ephron; and Abraham weighed to Ephron the Silver, which he had named in the hearing of the children of Heth, four hundred shekels of silver, current money with the merchant." (Gen 23:16)

On the question of why the Torah states the exact purchase price for the care of Machpela, R. Samuel Mohilever explains that it is to teach us a great lesson; "The Torah emphasized that there is no price too high for even the smallest portion of the land of Israel," as the burial cave was not worth close to what Abraham paid. This price, J. David Bleich explains, can be assessed not only in terms of currency, but in terms of a spiritual or emotional payment as well.[2] Does the Torah only teach us this lesson or does there exist a commandment to purchase the land of Israel? Numbers 33:53 states, "And ye shall drive out the inhabitants of the land and dwell within; for unto you have I given the land to possess it." Bleich explains in his book Contemporary Halakhic Problems – Vol. II, "The verse in question [according to Rambam] thus bids us 1) to conquer the land by force of arms; 2) to dwell in the land; 3) to refrain from seizing any other land; and 4) not to allow the land to remain in the hands of any other nation or allow it to remain desolate."[3] However, Rambam goes on to explain that this injunction does not constitute a binding obligation for all generations. Further, the Talmud, Ketubot IIIa declares that God causes the Jews to swear two solemn oaths-not to take the land of Israel by force and not to rebel against the nations of the world. In Vol. I of his book under the same title, Bleich explains that Rabbi Zevin does not support these Talmudic oaths. Rabbi Zevin explains that the Talmud records that these two oaths were accompanied by a third oath by the nations of the world – that they will not inordinately oppress Jews.[4] Persecution of the Jews by the third Reich, as well as the conditions of Jewry in the Soviet Union and South America have nullified this third oath, and thus, this releases the Jews from their side of the contract.

As the commandment to live in Israel is not included in Rambam's compilation of the 613 precepts, it is seen as a personal obligation, rather than a communal one. Of course, a person is relieved of this obligation if it places his life in danger. Dwelling in the West Bank, without returning this land, would certainly constitute danger to life. However, Rambam proclaims in Hikhot Avodat Kokhavim 10:6 that Jews are forbidden to sell houses or fields in Israel to a non-Jew, because it is written that you should not give them permanent property. Thus, the question of the return of the "administered territories" becomes one of semantics. Since the Arabs already have permanent residence, it is permissible to change the sovereignty of the land. There is no obligation to wage war for the conquest of the land of Israel or for the retention of the territories.[5]

Once we determine Halakhic standpoint on this issue, we must examine the Halakhic stand on its consequences. If we examine the political implications of the return of the West Bank, we determine that Halakha may not allow this solution to stand. Society has an obligation to prevent possible danger and loss of life as upheld in Baba Batra 76. If we view the Palestinian Liberation Organization as an instrument of Arab politics to create propaganda against

Israel, it can be understood that the return of the West Bank will be a danger to the security of Israel. The acquisition of yet more Arab territory would contribute to, as well as threaten the push of Israel into the sea. Is the State of Israel permitted to cause a threat to its own security? Likewise, is the state allowed to create conditions of a war by not taking any positive action in this matter? Both by returning the land and not returning it, the state of Israel shall be instigating a discretionary war or "milhemet reshut". What types of war does Halakha state are permissible for Israel to undertake? Certainly, Halakha allows any war commanded by the Torah, as well as a category of war "to diminish the heathens so that they shall not march against them." (Gemara on Deut 20:5-7). This category of war as understood by various translations of Rambam's "Commentary on the Mishna" includes war with an enemy that has been engaged in the taking of Jewish lives, military response to a war of attrition, war against nations that a state of belligerence already exists, and war against a nation when it is known they are building-up for attack.[6] Halakha thus views the State of Israel to withhold or return the West Bank, as both constitute a preemptive war sanctioned by Halakha.

What then, is our deciding factor? While retaining the land of Israel is a personal obligation, it is not considered a commandment for all generations, communally. Both the return of and the retention of the West Bank constitutes some form of passive preemptive war. And both the return and retention of the territories is threatening to the security of the State of Israel. Thus, the answer is retention. "You shall blot out the remembrance of Amalek" (Deut 25:19). Remember what Amalek did unto you" (Deut 25:17). Rambam explains, "By this injunction we are commanded that among the descendants of Esau, we are to exterminate only the seed of Amalek, male and female, young and old."[7] How do we determine the descendants of Amalek? R. Chaim Soloveitchik of Brisk declared that "the commandment to destroy Amalek extends not only to genealogical descendants of that ancient people, but encompasses all who embrace the ideology of Amalek and seek to annihilate the Jewish nation. Hence, the 'war of God against Amalek' continues from 'generation to generation' against the professed enemies of Israel, and in our day, is directed against those Arab nations which seek to eradicate the people of Israel."[8]

The Israeli government has decided too quickly to sacrifice Judaea and Samaria. Our chance of survival is far greater upon refusal to minimize our land, as reflected in these Halakhic interpretations. As it is written, "... I have set before you life and death, the blessing and the curse; therefor choose life, that thou may live, thou and thy seed." (Deut 30:19).

Glossary

Amalek – the first to attack Israel with the sword. The Torah imposes on us the obligation to accomplish his complete extermination. In Jewish tradition, the spirit of Amalek is the antithesis of and greatest hindrance to the manifestation of the reign of God in the World. (according to The Commandments)

Milhemet Reshut – Jewish law recognizes two distinct types of war: "milhemet mitsvah" or war commanded by the Torah and "milhemet reshut" or war that is not commanded by it permitted, and hence "discretionary." (according to "Tradition")

West Bank – the area of the "administered territories" constituting Judaea and Samaria, so called because it sits on the West side of the Jordan river

Notes

[1] Encyclopedia Judaica – Decennial Book (1973-1982) Keter Publishing, Jerusalem, p.92

[2] "Tradition" – Volume 18, No.1, (Summer, 1979). p.47. Rabbinical Council of America, NY. Judaea and Samaria: Settlement and Return. J. David Bleich. p.47

[3] Contemporary Halakhic Problems – Vol. II. Ktav Publishing House, NY, (1983). J. David Bleich. p.194

[4] Ibid – Vol. I p.15

[5] "Tradition" – Vol. 18, No. 1. p59

[6] "Tradition" – Vol. 21, No. 1 (Spring, 1983) p.12,13

[7] The Commandments – Sefer Ha-Mitzvot of Maimonidies. Transl. by Rabbi Dr. Charles B. Chavel. Soncino Press, London and NY. P.202

[8] Contemporary Halakhic Problems – Vol. I. p.17

Bibliography

The Commandments – Sefer Ha-Mitzvot of Maimonidies. Transl. by Rabbi Dr. Charles B. Chavel. (Soncino Press, London and NY) p.202

Contemporary Halakhic Problems – Vol. I. J. David Bleich (Ktav Publishing House, NY, 1983) p.15,17.

Contemporary Halakhic Problems – Vol. II. J. David Bleich (Ktav Publishing House, NY, 1983) p.194

Encyclopedia Judaica – Decennial Book (1973-1982) (Keter Publishing House, Jerusalem). p.92

"Tradition" – Volume 18, No. 1, (Summer, 1979) (Rabbinical Council of America, NY) Judaea and Samaria: Settlement and Return, J. David Bleich. p.47,59

"Tradition" – Volume 21, No 1, (Spring, 1983) (Rabbinical Council of America, NY). Preemptive War in Jewish Law. J. David Bleich. p.12,13

To put the previous paper into perspective, it is important to realize the geographical and population disparities between Israel and the surrounding Arab nations. 426 million more followers of Islam occupy 650 times more land, an estimated 76.7 times more people than Israel. According to Wikipedia, the total Islamic population of the world is 1.7 billion.

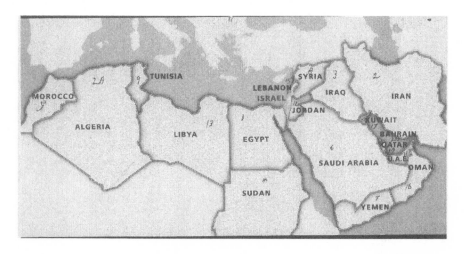

Number	Country	Population
1	Egypt	84,605,000
2	Iran	77,059,000
2A	Algeria	38,295,000
3	Iraq	35,404,000
4	Sudan	35,150,000
5	Morocco	32,950,000
6	Saudi Arabia	30,193,000
7	Yemen	25,252,000
8	Syria	22,169,000
9	Tunisia	10,889,000
10	Somalia	9,662,000
11	United Arab Emirates	8,659,000
12	Jordan	6,517,000
13	Libya	6,323,000
14	West Bank	4,421,000
15	Lebanon	4,127,000
16	Oman	3,942,000
17	Kuwait	3,852,000

| 19 | Qatar | 1,917,000 |
| 20 | Bahrain | 1,546,000 |

The disparity in area and population seems proportional to the disparity in UN resolutions against Israel, 77 versus 1 against the Palestinians. This also reflects the fact that anti-Semitism today is greater than ever in history and reveals humanity's bias against truth, justice, love, and mercy. Only a genuine return to our Jewish roots will change society's inevitable march toward a Jew free, godless world. God forbid.

A viable vehicle for cooperation with the Arab world is expressed in the following proposal, by Eric Lerner and others, regarding the joint development of fusion energy.

FUSION FOR PEACE

A PROPOSAL FROM US, IRANIAN AND JAPANESE PHYSICISTS FOR ENDING THE CONFRONTATION WITH IRAN

By Eric Lerner, Lawrenceville Plasma Physics, Inc.; Hamid Reza Yousef, I. Azad University; Morteza Habibi, Amirkabir University of Technology; Alireza Zaeem, Khaje Nasir University of Technology; Jun-Ichi Sakai, Toyama University; Takayuki Haruki, Toyama University

We are hearing it again: we need to attack a Mid-Eastern nation to prevent it from getting weapons of mass destruction. The war, we are told again, will be quick and easy – a surgical strike. Perhaps US troops don't even need to get involved – Israel will do the job. This time the target is Iran.

It may seem strange for the US, Israel, France, the UK, Russia or China, who have nuclear weapons in abundance, to be deciding that Iran must not have them. Setting that aside, we can all agree that it is desirable to stop the spread of nuclear weapons to more and more nations. But is yet another "pre-emptive" war the only way to achieve the goal? Does the path to peace really lie in using force to prevent a nation from going beyond dependence on oil and gas?

As physicists in Iran, Japan and the US, we are proposing an alternative: starting a scientific and engineering collaboration effort between the countries that could, if successful, make uranium enrichment obsolete, block proliferation everywhere, liberate the world from oil and coal, and open up a new source of cheap, clean, unlimited energy. In the past three years, Iran has become a major player in the small but growing global effort to achieve aneutronic fusion power – controlled nuclear fusion using fuels that produce no neutrons. Controlled fusion harnesses the power that heats the sun – nuclear fusion – as a source of energy for peaceful purposes. Fuels that don't produce neutrons are important because neutrons can be extremely destructive, damaging the structure of a fusion generator and inducing radioactivity.

Most of the world's effort in controlled fusion has aimed at using deuterium-tritium (DT) fuel, which produces large numbers of high-energy neutrons, unlike aneutronic fuels. DT-based fusion devices must necessarily be very large for a given power, to dilute the damage done by the neutrons to a manageable level. As a result, (and also due to their complexity and other factors), such devices are also very expensive to build, costing billions of dollars and taking many years or even decades to build. This has been one factor, among others, that has made the pursuit of such DT fusion energy so slow and hard.

By contrast, aneutronic fusion devices can be quite compact and cheap as they don't need to withstand intense neutron bombardment. Some, like a device called the dense plasma focus (DPF), can be built for hundreds of thousands of dollars while others, called inertial electrical confinement devices (IEC), cost a few million. Iran's controlled fusion program has focused on these economical aneutronic devices in an attempt to leapfrog over DT-fusion to get a cheap, clean and inexhaustible energy source. Already, Iran has set up more active DPF research groups – six – than any other country in the world. The United States is the only other country with an active aneutronic fusion effort.

Aneutronic fusion could make uranium enrichment obsolete because, if it works, aneutronic-fusion-produced electricity would be cheaper than any available today. Aneutronic fuels produce energy that can be converted directly into electricity, without going through the expensive cycle of generating steam and putting it through turbines. Such an ideal energy source would be far cheaper than nuclear fission energy based on uranium, (what is commonly called nuclear energy). There would be no reason for Iran or any other country to continue to pursue fission energy for peaceful purposes. To prevent nuclear weapon proliferation, the use of uranium could be universally banned as nuclear fission energy production was shut down.

The catch in all this is that aneutronic fusion requires temperatures even higher than those for DT fusion – billions of degrees – five to ten times hotter than is needed for DT fusion, and these fuels burn slower than DT. That is the reason that fusion efforts have focused on DT, despite the much larger expense. Aneutronic fusion just seemed too difficult. Yet in the past year this has changed. Research reported in respected peer-reviewed scientific journals has shown that the temperature needed to ignite aneutronic fuels has been achieved and confined. At the same time, research by both US and Iranian fusion scientists have confirmed theoretically that aneutronic fusion could be achieved by DPFs, IECs and perhaps, table-top-sized ultra-short-pulse lasers. In light of these new scientific developments, and of the real threat of war between the US and Iran, we are proposing the establishment of a joint US-Iran Aneutronic Fusion Program, to accelerate this research and pool the resources of the various aneutronic projects. Unlike DT-fusion, aneutronic devices can be built in months, not decades, so a joint program could quickly determine if aneutronic fusion can work. If it can, a prototype generator could be built within a few years, at a cost of perhaps $200 million, an insignificant fraction of the devastating costs of a new war.

The program would aim to rapidly establish two Aneutronic Fusion Centers, one in the US and one in Iran, staffed by scientists and engineers from both countries and funded by the governments in proportion to their respective national GDPs. These Centers would work in cooperation with existing research groups, but with greater resources could speed up the work several-fold. Research results would be fully shared by the two countries. As the project grows, other countries not now involved in aneutronic work can join in the establishment of the project, which itself will ease tensions between the two countries. If it succeeds, in a few years, all uranium enrichment for energy production would be obsolete and could be shut down not just in Iran, but everywhere. This would be a giant step to ending nuclear proliferation worldwide. And as aneutronic fusion supersedes fossil fuels, they would remove oil as the real fuel of the decades-long tension and wars in the Middle-East.

There is a risk that aneutronic fusion will take much longer than we think, despite recent encouraging advances. But the risks of war are far greater than the risks of trying to eliminate the causes of war. And the potential rewards-both for peace and for the development of a cheap, clean energy source that can replace both fossil and fission-are enormous. We call on scientists in both countries, as well as all who want a route out of the dead-end of war, all who want to see if there is another route to clean energy, to join together to make this route a reality.

We are on the verge of a paradigm shift in the way we power the world. Pollution free, environmentally safe, inexhaustible energy will be available soon. Small plants capable of powering 5000 homes for 5 years at a cost of about $350,000 should be available within 5 years. That is about a tenth of the price of coal and with no pollution. It will enable replacement of all coal-fired plants and the outlawing of uranium production. Ultimately, uranium has only one practical use: the making of atomic weapons. (I am on the board of advisors of Lawrenceville Plasma Physics and own stock in that company. Its website is available to any interest parties)

The independent Lawrenceville Plasma Physics (LPP) technology review committee was pleasantly surprised by the efforts and progress made by LPP in its development of the Dense Plasma Focus (DPF) fusion power concept. While recent progress has been notable, significant physics issues as well as a number of engineering challenges remain to be addressed before the practical viability of the concept can be fully evaluated. The committee found that LPP has identified some major physics challenges to achieving aneutronic fusion with a DPF and formulated a near-term program to address them.

174

More information can be found at http://www.LPPFusion.com.

CONCLUSION

77 UN resolutions against Israel and only one against the Palestinians show the extreme bias of the UN and the inability of the United States to influence their decision making process. It is time to move the UN out of the United States and for Israel to declare itself a single Jewish state from the mountains to the sea. This will require that Israel develop a constitution, declaring the same. Jews and Palestinians should be allowed to live wherever they want in that state, serve in the army, and otherwise enjoy all the privileges of citizenship. Disloyalty or attacks against the nation of Israel should result in immediate expulsion of the perpetrator and their family.

It should be obvious to anyone that there is no negotiating with the Arab world and it is long past time to attempt to do so. The Arab world sees only one resolution and that involves destruction of the Jewish

State. From personal discussions, I know that some Israelis would be uncomfortable with this prospect and the few Palestinians I have spoken with think that would be a wonderful idea. My personal experience has shown that the Palestinians were the primary workers who developed the oil fields in the Arab countries and are intelligent and industrious workers.

I believe if treated with those expectations, they will respond accordingly and of course, those Palestinians now living in Israel have set an example which should make the case, or not. Regardless, they should accept citizenship or be prepared to leave. No other resolution seems possible based on the years of experience since 1948.

I have been told by prominent Israelis that this is not a viable solution, and living in America I am not qualified to speak on their behalf. But as they are threatened, I am threatened. In light of the internecine warfare, there does not appear to be any viable option. Strength and force is the message the Arab world most clearly understands and anything less is tantamount to surrender.

That spells finis to my effort to save the world.

Chaim Wolff

Chaim Wolff

ACKNOWLEDGEMENT

To my wife Madilyn, my greatest love and respect for putting up with my unceasing search for truth, which validates my love for you.

Thanks to Baron LeBourgeois for his technical assistance.

Supplemental Bibliography

Sherwin, Byron L., "Towards a Jewish Theology," The Edward Mellon Press. pg. 9

Heschel, Abraham, Joshua, God in search of man. pgs. 414, 246

Jacobs, Louis, "A Jewish Theology," pg. 126, 129.

Sherwin, Byron L., "Toward a Jewish Theology," pgs. 86, 89

Jewish Theology Background Readings, Volume 2, pg. 416

The Jerusalem Post, June 28, 1997 "America Do It Yourself Torah" pg. 19

Bernard J. Lee, "The Galilean Jewishness of Jesus" A Stimulus Book, Paulist Press, 1988 Bernardino, J. (Cardinal), *Christian Anti-Semitism: A History of Hate,* pg. XVII: Avonson 1993, pgs. 413-415, 429-430

Mussner, Franz, "Tractate on the Jews," p. VII, Fortress/Spck, 1984

Class Notes, Jose Faur, "The Rabbinic Mind."

Bickerman, Elias J., "The Jews" Volume 1, pgs. 70, 73, 76

Faur, Jose "Monolingualism and Judaism." Cardoza Law Review, Volume 14: pgs.1713, 1724, 1730.

Bickerman, Elias J., pg. 94.

Faur, Jose. "Golden Doves with Silver Dots," pgs. 85, 86, 90, 116, 120, 134.

Faur, Jose, "Monolingualism and Judaism" pgs. 1713, 1714, 1719

Faur, Jose. "Journal of Jewish Studies" Volume 28, pgs. 37, 39, 40, 42, 43

Faur, Jose. "Doves" pg. 145.

Kaufmann, Y. The Religion of Israel

Kaplan, Schwartz, "A psychology of hope", Praeger

Nicholls, William, "Christian Antisemitism," A History of Hate, Aronson

Baeck, Leo, "Judaism and Christianity," Athenaeum

Zinburg, Israel, A History of Jewish Literature, Volume 2, Case

Western Reserve University Press, 1972, pgs. 11, 14

Hyman Arthur, "Philosophy, Jewish," Encyclopedia Judaica, Volume 13, page 438.

Jacobs, Louis, "Jewish Biblical Exegesis," Berhman House, 1973, page 8, 9, 10, 11, 14, 16, 59.

Holtz Berry, "Back to the Sources," Summit Books, pages 216, 254-256, 228-229, 308, 309-310, 314, 319, 320-329, 376, 384-385.

Talmadge, Frank, "Apples of Gold," in Arthur Green, E.D., Jewish Spirituality (New York: Crossroad Publishing Co.), pg. 325.

Jacobs, Louis, Jewish Law, New York: pp. 120, 121, 122.

Twersky, Isadore, The Shulhan Aruch: Enduring Code of Jewish Law, "Judaism" 16:2 (Spring, 1967) pgs. 122, 142, 143, 144, 145.

Elliot N. Dorff and Arthur Rosett, A Living Tree, The Roots and Growth of Jewish Law. Albany, New York: State University of New York Press, pp.375-377, 383-387, 392.

Sherwin, Byron L. and Cohen, Seymour J., "How to be a Jew." Northvale, New Jersey; Jason Henson, Inc., 1992.

Joseph, Dan, "Ethical Literature," Vol. VI., pg. 930. Encyclopedia, Judaica,

Bahya ben Joseph Ibn pakudah. The Book of Direction to the Duties of the Heart. London: Routledge and Kegan Paul, 1973.

Moses Khayyam Luzzatto. Mesillat Yesharim - The Path of the Upright.

Solomon Ibn Gabirol, "Choice of Pearls", New York; Block Publishing Co., Inc. 1925; pgs. 25, 26, 27.

Rudavsky David, "Modem Jewish Religious Moments," Behrman House, Inc. pgs.9, 35, 175-177, 312, 316

Meyer, Michael A. "Response to Modernity" Oxford University Press, pgs. 13, 53, 295.

Neusner, Jacob "Understanding American Judaism" KT A V Publishing House, Inc. pgs. 7, 8, 272, 273.

Gillman, Neil "Conservative Judaism" Behrman House, pgs. 43, 59, 62, 74, 76, 79, 79, 119.

Elias, Joseph. "The Nineteen Letters" Feldheim Publishers, pgs. 2, 4-6, 12, 20, 27, 33, 33, 58, 77, 109, 144, 146, 201, 274.

http://www.lynellen.comlwrite/torah.html

Barlow, Sir James, - Review of the book entitled: The Bodacious Descendant by Darrell Swanson, © 2010

Leonard Susskind, December 1, 2006, The Cosmic Landscape: String Theory and the Illusion of Intelligent Design, pgs. 61, 62.

John Leslie, Universe - Evidence of Fine Tuning, pg. 29.

J.P. Moreland, Editor, 1994, The Creation Hypothesis: Scientific Evidence for an Intelligent Designer, InterVarsity Press, Downers Grove, IL, pgs. 160-171, 282, 283, 287, 288, 292.

http://www.ivpress.comlcgi-ivpress/book.pl/code = 1698

Ankerberg, John & Weldon, John, Appendix - Rational inquiry & the force of scientific data: Are new Horizons Emerging? pgs. 270-272.

Evolution I, Tom Space: A Theory of Cosmic Creationism, Sir Fred Hoyle, Chandra Wickramasinghe, Simon & Schuster (Paper); 1st edition (January 1984)

Hawking, Stephen & Mlodinow, Leonard, *The Grand Design,* Batam Books, 2010 - reviews

Michael Holden (2010-09-02). "God did not create the universe, says Hawking". Reuters. http://ea.news. yahoo.com/s/reuters/1 00902/science/science _us _ britain_hawking. Retrieved 2010-10-17

Patai, Rafael, "The Arab Mind," Scribners 1973

Novak, Michael, The Spirit of Democratic Capitalism - An American Enterprise Institute, Simon & Shuster Publication, pgs. 13-21, 31-36, 56, 70, 71, 122, 123, 242.

Voegeli, William, Commentary Magazine, June 2011 issue - pgs. 36, 90, 91, 124, 350-352

Caritas. The highest of all theological symbols for Judaism and Christianity is the one closest to the personality of God: compassion, sacrificial love - Caritas is the proper name of the Creator, pgs. 242, 357

The Two Trillion Dollar Meltdown - Bubble Land: Practice Runs - Foreword, pgs. XIV, XV, XVII, XVIII, pgs. 44, 45, 68-69, 146, 152-153,158, 159

US-Israel Bond, Ambassador (ret.) Yoram Ettinger, "Second Thought: US-Israel Initiative" Pajamas Media, July 15, 2011.

Isaac Jewels, "The Teaching of Contempt: Christian Roots of Anti-Semitism", Holt, Reinhardt & Houston, New York, 1964, pg. 29.

Isaac Jewels, pg. 39.

Jesus, Rabbi and Lord: The Hebrew Story of Jesus Behind Our Gospels, Cornerstone Pub; 1st edition (August 1989)

Franklin H. Littell, The Anabaptist View of the Church (Dissent and Nonconformity) The Baptist Standard Bearer (April 6, 2001)

Fisher, Eugene J., Faith without Prejudice (A Deus book) Paulist Press International, U.S. (December 1977)

Pirke Avot, Chapter 1, Siddur Sim Shalom, The United Synagogue of America, 1985, pg. 603.

Flannery, Edward H., Anguish of the Jews: twenty-three centuries of anti-Semitism, Macmillan (1971)

Eckardt and Eckardt, Encounter with Israel, pgs. 229-231

Another book by Chaim Wolff

ABOUT THE AUTHOR

Chaim Wolff grew up in a small town in Arkansas, worked in his father's junkyard, became the highest ranking cadet in Western Military Academy's history, graduated from the University of Illinois with a triple degree in chemistry, geology, and civil engineering, then built a career as a drilling engineer and became the staff advisor to Shell Oil Companies Deep Drilling Study group. His drilling engineering phase included drilling operations through every major geologic section; from the earliest settlements in the Gulf of Mexico to the oldest sediments, including penetration of the Earth's mantle in order to communicate with what was then a top-secret project involving the United States' submarine fleet.

While acting as an advisor to the study group for Shell, he discovered a source of iron oxide uniquely suited for use in drilling and production operations. He subsequently left Shell to pursue this business opportunity which subsequently grew into the Sulfatreat Company, which was later sold to the Schlumberger Company. During that work experience he traveled worldwide and to some places which had never seen a white person. In 1974 that included the interior of China to "the village of long life". That required flying in an old C 47 which had traveled "the Hump". It was filled with Chinese peasants wearing their Mao jackets who are as amazed with him as he with them. The stewardess was brewing tea over an open Bunsen burner!

The trip over land required a six-hour jeep ride over unimproved roads, covered with rocks from a rock crusher (the most advanced piece of machinery he saw). The boulders to feed this crusher were carried by two people, a woman and a man with a sling between them who handled a load he estimated at more than 200 pounds. The only job reserved for women was "honeypot carriers" the contents of which were used to fertilize the rice fields.

The rice that was served at 6 AM and again at 6 PM was contained in a single small bowl and appeared to him to be the only food for the day. At the end of the day he would take his usual jog and by the time he returned the roads were lined with mothers bringing their children to see the very old giant. Face-to-face was experienced when traveling in public. They had never seen a white man before.

This is the country, which we believe is the key to our future. They hold so much of our debt. In his opinion it is on the verge of a national calamity caused by its restrictive birth practices, centralized ideological planning and communist rule." The little Red Book" describes the road to ruin. They need our help far more than we need theirs, now that we have gotten our act together. With the opportunity that the preceding presented, he attended Spertus College and obtained 33 hours of credit toward a master's degree in Jewish studies.

His first book "The Lord our God is truth" was a labor of love and this book includes the most important information from that one. By way of explanation this biography establishes his credentials to comment on the state of the world as he sees it. The books title "The Critical Path" is based upon an oilfield practice required before bidding on an offshore lease. This practice required the evaluation of hundreds or even thousands of individual tasks which needed to be completed by dozens or hundreds of individual participants in order to be prepared to install a platform offshore within 3 to 5 years and before an initial bid for the lease had been prepared.

Paul, we are one big collective able to make the world manifest God's will. It will require a return to our Jewish roots as exemplified by Jesus. We are both on that road.

Enjoy spending time with you and Gene.

Rabbi Chaim White

Made in the USA
Charleston, SC
20 January 2017